TURNING THE TABLES ON MISSION

Stories of Christians from the global south in the UK

Edited by
Rev Israel Oluwole Olofinjana

instant
apostle

First published in Great Britain in 2013

Instant Apostle
The Hub
3-5 Rickmansworth Road
Watford
Herts
WD18 OGX

British Library Cataloguing-in-Publication Data

A catalogue record for this book is available from the British Library

This book and all other Instant Apostle books are available from Instant Apostle:

Website: www.instantapostle.com
E-mail: info@instantapostle.com

ISBN 978-1-909728-03-5

Printed in Great Britain

Instant Apostle is a new way of getting ideas flowing, between followers of Jesus, and between those who would like to know more about His Kingdom.

It's not just about books and it's not about a one-way information flow. It's about building a community where ideas are exchanged. Ideas will be expressed at an appropriate length. Some will take the form of books. But in many cases ideas can be expressed more briefly than in a book. Short books, or pamphlets, will be an important part of what we provide. As with pamphlets of old, these are likely to be opinionated, and produced quickly so that the community can discuss them.

Well-known authors are welcome, but we also welcome new writers. We are looking for prophetic voices, authentic and original ideas, produced at any length; quick and relevant, insightful and opinionated. And as the name implies, these will be released very quickly, either as Kindle books or printed texts or both.

Join the community. Get reading, get writing and get discussing!

Contents

Commendations

It was approaching Christmas 2004 when a young Nigerian entered the church I pastor in south east London. Little did I realise the impact this man would have on our church and my ministry. Israel impressed us with his humility, his Bible knowledge, his willingness to learn and his ability to teach. By 2007 we were pastoring the church together. Israel brought a confidence in the gospel that challenged us and moved us on. We changed the structures of our house groups, we became bolder in our sharing of the gospel, we became excited about digging deep into the Old Testament and applying the lessons to our lives. Israel and I learned to work together, to see things from each other's perspective and respect other ways of doing church.

As I have read the stories contained in this book I have again been humbled and challenged. The stories of these modern missionaries are inspiring. Here are stories of men and women who had to combat racism and discouragement, and did so with humility, perseverance and a sure confidence in their God. These stories of God at work and faith in action should spur us all on, as together we pray, Your kingdom come, Your will be done here as it is in heaven.

I commend this book to you.

Rev Carol Bostridge, Pastor of Crofton Park Baptist Church

Reverse mission, as missionaries from other parts of the world pursue their vocation to re-evangelise Britain and plant new kinds of churches, is a hugely significant development that indigenous British Christians will be wise to welcome, interact with and learn from. This collection of stories and reflections is an excellent resource for such interaction and learning.

Rev Dr Stuart Murray Williams, Founder of Urban Expression

Turning the Tables on Mission: Stories of Christians from the global south in the UK is an important contribution to the growing body of

literature exploring the changing face of Christianity in contemporary Britain. The influential role of Christians from the global south is proving to be one of the most significant and transformative elements in the British religious landscape. Yet while many studies treat world Christianity in isolation from British Christian networks, one of the great strengths of *Turning the Tables on Mission* is that it points to the increasing connections and shared identities between diasporic Christians in this country and British 'indigenes', demonstrating that we are increasingly observing a transformation *within* British Christianity rather than merely a foreign addition to it. Additionally, the volume's focus on the autobiographical stories of individual church leaders and planters offers readers rich and nuanced accounts of the motivations, desires and challenges that prompt this remarkable group of individuals.
Dr Joel Cabrita, Department of Theology and Religious Studies, University of Cambridge

There can be no greater need in an increasingly complex society than for the Christian Church to rediscover and renew its mission in the world. Being God's light, salt and leaven bespeaks an incarnational existence that does not settle for mere coexistence, but one that transforms its context. Any initiative that helps in this task is to be welcomed, and I particularly welcome Rev Olofinjana's bringing together of experts and practitioners from south and north to reflect upon the Church's mission and what one part of the body of Christ can learn from another as together we seek to bring the good news of God's salvation to our world.
Bishop Dr Joe Aldred, Secretary, Minority Ethnic Christian Affairs (MECA), Churches Together in England (CTE)

On 15th September 2010 at the Evangelical Alliance UK Council meeting, following a short address by Bishop Wilton Powell (National Overseer, Church of God of Prophecy) and Pastor Agu Irukwu (Senior Pastor, Jesus House), there occurred what I can only describe as a powerful God moment. Men and women were on their knees responding to God and recognising His challenge to find a fresh expression of unity which crossed all ethnic divides. This was a call to unity in the midst of our diversity. A unity for a purpose, expressed in the great prayer of John 17:21, 'that the world may believe'. The Evangelical Alliance, I trust, will never be the same. A 'One People Commission' is now working to see this reflected in every area of our work.

This book tells some of the stories of a God movement which is impacting the church right across the UK. I thank God for the gift He is giving to us at this time.

Steve Clifford, General Director, Evangelical Alliance

These stories make fascinating yet challenging reading. The common thread is the certainty of a plea from the authors for the recognition of their calling, including culture, personality and difference. Their primary and genuine desire is to be obedient to God. There is also a call to partake in the work that God is doing and a recognition that both black- and white-majority churches and their leaders need to cast aside scepticism and learn from each other. As I read these stories, it was as if I was reading my own story, and no doubt countless people will feel the same. The challenge therefore is to listen to the integrity of these leaders. Let our hearts be transformed and, most of all, embrace enthusiastically the needs for mission here in Britain far more than overseas.

Mark Sturge, London Region, Head of Christian Aid

The number of Christians who have moved from the global south to the UK is growing all the time. Why have they come? What do they find? What is their impact? The answers are varied and complex, and the value of this book is in the telling of the personal stories of those who have made the journey. Each, naturally, is different, but all offer a wealth of insight. This is an invaluable resource to anyone seeking to deepen their understanding of reverse missionaries, cross-cultural mission – and quite simply, the language of spiritual friendship.

Paul Hobson, Editor of *The Baptist Times*

This is a very interesting and worthwhile text. The stories of men and women of faith coming from all over the world to witness and preach the gospel in the United Kingdom is a story that needs to be told, and this book is an important contribution in the telling of those stories. This collection forces us to reorientate our gaze and to see new and older ethnic minority communities in the UK as major assets to the church and society. For that reason it deserves to be read, discussed and shared.

Dr William Ackah, Birkbeck, University of London

The last 50 years has been a time of phenomenal change in Western society, and we're not finished yet. During this period and to the present day, a quiet revolution is taking place. As the population in the UK has disengaged from the Christian faith, so the church of the global south has appeared in our midst. Have we the wisdom to understand what might be happening, and the humility to see that God is doing a new thing in our nation?

Israel Olofinjana has gathered together stories that capture the essence of a turnaround in our understanding of how mission is happening today. This book tells the stories of missionary enterprises that start in the places once seen as the great mission fields of the world, and have as their destination one of the great mission sending centres – the United Kingdom. Only God knows the future, but I believe the day is coming when our generation will be spoken of as the time when one of the great paradigm shifts in global mission took place.

David Kerrigan, General Director, Baptist Missionary Society

The mission historian Andrew Walls speaks of the 'Ephesian moment' when two different first-century cultures came together to experience Christ. In twenty-first-century Britain, particularly in our cities, we are in an Ephesian moment again. Now it is a kaleidoscope of cultures, but the words of Ephesians still hit the mark – the church is 'being built together' in the Spirit (Ephesians 2:22). Embedding this theology in lived experience, these stories capture something of the growing pains of this moment. Originating in the global south, the contributors are honest about the challenges and struggles they have faced in coming to live in Britain, yet they also inspire as they testify to the reality of seeing God at work.

Overturning preconceptions about where mission is 'from' and 'to', the voices we hear in this book may not be easy listening for British churches, but we need to tune in. Such voices make it plain that we have a lot to learn from each other.

Dr Andrew Rogers, Being Built Together, University of Roehampton, London

This commendable publication provides a very engaging description and reflection on the formative journey of 12 contemporary pilgrims from the global south and their impact on the church in the UK. The stories offer some insightful models to aide our understanding of the call to mission and Christian leadership in our time, and in so doing present gentle challenges about how we embrace and demonstrate God's purposes in and for our world.

Phyllis Thompson, Education Director, New Testament Church of God Leadership Training Centre

Israel Olofinjana has produced a very valuable contribution to the debate about reverse missions. Among all the theory, he has written definitive empirical accounts of several pioneers. Their stories illustrate just what is involved in reverse mission, the challenges and the opportunities. There is much to learn from in this book, which both experienced pastors and those considering a call might consider carefully. This historic development in the British church scene possesses many admirable new initiatives. On the other hand, there is also much naivety, among both incomers who do not understand the British context, and indigenous leaders who unrealistically see this as the solution to dwindling congregations. Israel Olofinjana's own careful evaluative comments on the phenomenon helpfully guide us to make the most of the growth of new churches in Britain. He enables us to avoid falling prey to over-optimistic illusions, but without giving up hope for God's future move in revival in the United Kingdom.

Rev Dr Steve Latham, Spurgeon's College

Historians are currently rediscovering the importance and value of 'telling stories'. The personal narratives compiled in this book are not only inspiring and thought provoking for those actively working in Christian ministry, but they are also a valuable resource for those of us who are seeking to understand and interpret the past, and to appreciate how migration and 'reverse mission' are reshaping churches in the present-day United Kingdom and transforming their relationship to the wider world. They serve as a stimulus to academics and practitioners to work together to collect more such accounts and to draw out their implications and practical applications for the future.

Prof John Wolffe, Professor of Religious History, The Open University

David Bosch in his seminal book *Transforming Mission* refers to the many paradigm shifts that take place in mission, and what we see taking place now is one such example. Furthermore, he proposes that there is a 'pluriverse' understanding of mission, and similarly there is a 'pluriverse' flow of peoples taking the gospel from different parts of the world to other different parts of the world. What is possibly unique in these stories is that those coming to Britain and other Western nations do not carry with them the inherent belief that they are the carriers of a superior culture and faith, which was so much a part of Western missionary endeavours. Instead, many come reluctantly and unwillingly; they echo the words of the apostle Paul, who wrote, 'I came to you in weakness with great fear and trembling' (1 Corinthians 2:3). I pray that these stories will inspire and encourage us to not rely on who we are but on who God is, His power and wisdom, as we seek to make Christ known in post-Christian Britain.

Rev Kumar Rajagopalan, Racial Justice Coordinator, London Baptist Association

The greatest need of the church, as we attempt to meet the challenges of the twenty-first century, is to engage with each other to propagate the 'good news' to the peoples of the world. There is no greater context in which this can be facilitated than around the great commission of mission. The efforts of Rev Olofinjana and others in highlighting the transformational power of mission, particularly when carried out together, is commendable and an important contribution to the body of literature exploring the changing face of mission in postmodern Britain.

Rev N. J. Sterling, International Executive Secretary and Director of Studies at The Institute of Theology & Christian Counselling, the New Testament Assembly

The vivid narratives of Christians from the global South in Britain that are documented in this book are a testament to the resurgence of Christianity in Britain partly through immigrant communities; the growing diversification of the British religious landscape; and the new agency and harbingers of the reverse mission process from the two-thirds world. These interesting tales are not simple stories in themselves, they point to ways in which we can begin to chart emergent theologies of immigrant Christian communities in Britain through personal life encounters, experiences and expressions. I warmly recommend it to all who are interested in understanding the complexity of contemporary Christian mission and transcultural encounters.

Dr Afe Adogame, The University of Edinburgh

This book is far more than a collection of mini biographies. Each contributor not only shares their own spiritual journey with honesty and insight, but they also raise a range of thought-provoking analyses of topics related to vision for mission, the challenges of multicultural church, unity respecting cultural differences and the impact of prejudice and racism. Rev Olofinjana highlights and comments on these topics in his reflections throughout the book and has also contributed detailed historical research and references. It is therefore both academic and accessible because of its personal narrative style. It features a well-chosen selection of contributors whose faith, vision and resilience in the face of problems and experiences of God are inspirational. This book is relevant to both scholars and practitioners who want to understand more about the reality of 'reverse mission'. It will also be a helpful companion for the ministers and missionaries from churches in the global south who will hear the call of God to come to Britain and help extend the kingdom of God.

Claire Siddaway, Former Coordinator, Latin Partners

Rev Olofinjana is one of only a few African writers engaged in the painstaking work of researching, documenting and charting the trajectory of Christianity both on the African continent and here in the UK, delineating the tensions and convergences in theology, spirituality and cultures. The value and significance of this work will only be realised as future generations seek to gaze retrospectively, attempting to find out what the Holy Spirit is doing in the present by understanding the past. This collection of first-person biographical accounts is another worthwhile contribution, and I welcome it as such!

Rev David Shosanya, Regional Minister, London Baptist Association

Profile of contributors

Tayo Arikawe is a missionary and Bible teacher. One of his recent interests is reverse mission with a view to building multicultural churches that will reach out to the lost in the continent of Europe. He is the International Director of Grace Evangelistic Ministries Europe (GEM),  a non-denominational Bible-teaching missionary organisation whose first priority is to take the gospel of grace to a lost and dying world. The ministry operates in more than 60 countries of the world. Tayo is currently writing his MTh dissertation at the University of Chester via Wales Evangelical School of Theology. On a good day, he will be found at the gym. He is married to Calista and they are blessed with one son, Mekus.

 **Rev Rodrigo Assis da Silva** was born and raised in Santos-SP, Brazil. He holds a BA in Theology from the Theological Baptist College of Sao Paulo and an MA in Religious Education from King's College London. He worked for the Brazilian Air Force for almost five years before going into full-time Baptist ministry. Rodrigo had the opportunity to serve God in three different continents in the first years of his ministry: as a trainee pastor in Brazil and as a missionary in Mozambique and Wales. He later served as a pastor in England where he worked for five years, first as an assistant minister at Emmanuel Baptist Church Thamesmead and later as an interim pastor at Woolwich Central Baptist Church – both multicultural churches in south-east London. He currently serves as the senior pastor at Bethel International Baptist Church – a multicultural English-speaking church in

Frankfurt, Germany. Pastor Rodrigo is happily married to the social worker and family therapist Annalena Assis da Silva.

Dotha N. Blackwood was born and educated in Jamaica and was converted to Christianity in 1977. She worked in Kingston, Jamaica, for the Jamaica Citizens Bank Ltd and as a director of the International Accelerated Missions (IAM) Bible School while freelancing as a drummer. In 1993, Dotha moved to England as director of the IAM Bible School in London. She was also a church leader with New Life Assembly, Dalston, from 1994 to 1997 before becoming an  associate minister at the Dulwich branch. Dotha is a graduate of Spurgeon's College, having achieved a Masters in Christian Doctrine after successfully completing her BD (Hons) there. She is also a graduate of the Jamaica School of Music where she studied, played and taught drums and other percussion instruments. Over the years, Dotha has been a minister of music and a worship leader at various conferences, and has led many worship seminars and been the choir director of a 100-voice choir for ten years. She currently lectures in Practical Theology at Spurgeon's College.

 **Rev Joel Edwards** is the International Director of Micah Challenge, a global Christian response to extreme poverty, having been their co-chair from 2004 to 2007. Prior to his role within Micah Challenge, Joel was General Director of the Evangelical Alliance UK, a post he held for more than ten years. He has also been the general secretary of the African and Caribbean Evangelical Alliance (ACEA). Joel is committed to harmonising matters of faith in the public square, and advocating on behalf of the world's poor.

Dr Ram Gidoomal CBE is a successful businessman and entrepreneur who over the last 20 years has used his business acumen to support the work of numerous public and charitable organisations and global and local missions. In 2011 he was appointed Chairman of Traidcraft. He is Chair of the Office of the Independent Adjudicator for Higher Education for  England and Wales, South Asian Concern, Allia and Future Business. He is a board member of the International Justice Mission, a fellow of the Royal Society of Arts and a visiting professor of entrepreneurship at Middlesex University. Ram is also a freeman of the City of London, a liveryman of the Worshipful Company of Information Technologists and a companion of the Chartered Management Institute. Past roles include UK Chief Executive of the Inlaks Group, Crown appointee to the Court and Council of Imperial College London and founder of the Christmas Cracker Charity which has raised more than £5 million and engaged more than 50,000 young people. He was a candidate for London Mayor for the Christian Peoples Alliance in 2000 and 2004, gaining nearly 100,000 votes in each election. He has written several books, including *Sari 'n' Chips*; *Chapatis for tea*; *Lions, Princesses and Gurus*; *The UK Maharajahs*; *The British and how to deal with them – Doing business with Britain's ethnic minorities* and *How would Jesus vote?*

 **Pastor José Carlos Lara** and his wife Mari Lara are Brazilian missionaries in Northern Ireland. They both received training in cross-cultural mission at CEM Centro Evangelico de Missoes in Brazil, and were involved in a church plant in their home nation. Pastor José was ordained as a Baptist minister in 1996 in Brazil. In 2004, he and his family answered God's call to be Latin Link missionaries in Northern Ireland. He later studied for an MA in Pastoral Theology at the Irish Baptist College, validated by the University of Wales. He

and Mari started a church for immigrants in Dungannon, Northern Ireland, in order to reach out to the ethnic minorities in that area. They are currently working with Christian Fellowship Church (CFC) in Belfast. They have three daughters who have also been involved in their missionary journeys.

Rev Israel Oluwole Olofinjana is a Baptist minister who pastored Crofton Park Baptist Church before becoming the pastor of Catford Community Church in September 2011, both in south-east London. He is Nigerian and comes from a Pentecostal background. He holds a BA (Hons) in Religious Studies from the University of Ibadan, Nigeria, and an MTh from Carolina University of Theology. Israel is the author of *Reverse in Ministry and Missions: Africans in the Dark Continent of Europe* (2010) and *20 Pentecostal Pioneers in Nigeria* (2011). He has also contributed to academic journals, magazines, conferences and seminars on the subject of black majority churches (BMC) in Britain and African Christianity. He was part of the council of reference of *Being Built Together*, a research project looking into the history and practices of BMCs in Southwark. He is also one of the Ecumenical Borough Deans in Lewisham working with the civic authorities. Israel blogs at israelolofinjana.wordpress.com and has recently established Centre for Missionaries from the Majority World. He is happily married to Lucy.

Dr Jonathan Oloyede is the Convener of London's Global Day of Prayer. His vision is to see the United Kingdom saturated with prayer. Jonathan and his wife Abi are the pastors of City Chapel in Beckton after having pastored at Glory House for more than a decade. Born in Britain but bred in Nigeria, Dr Oloyede is a medical doctor by profession and was called as a missionary to

England and Europe. He was radically saved from Islam within the wake of the revival that hit the Nigerian universities in the 1980s. He responded to God's call to be a missionary in Europe in 1991 while on a three-month holiday in London when the Holy Spirit visited him with a clear message. He is still here on that 'holiday'!

Peter Oyugi hails from Kenya and is currently the African Inland Mission (AIM) Mobiliser for the South of England and South Wales. Before this he was the pastor of Elmfield Church, a Free Evangelical Church in London. He studied Electrical and Communications Engineering at Moi University, Kenya, and later obtained a Masters Degree in Global Issues in Contemporary Mission at Redcliffe College, Gloucester. He served as a student worker for more than 11 years in Kenya and the UK, working for both the Fellowship of Christian Unions (FOCUS) in Kenya and the Universities and Colleges Christian Fellowship (UCCF), UK, on secondment. These are both part of the International Fellowship of Evangelical Students (IFES). Peter still teaches the Bible, often at IFES conferences in English-speaking Africa. He also served as a Careforce volunteer at St Luke's Church, Thurnby, Leicestershire for a year in 1995–6. He has a passion for cross-cultural mission that has grown out of being exposed to different cultures from childhood. Peter's father is Kenyan and his mother is Finnish. He is an avid sports lover and takes a keen interest in African politics. He is married to Cecilia and they have two daughters.

Harry Tennakoon was born into a Buddhist family in Sri Lanka, in a village called Galapitagala in the Anuradhapura District. He was a marketer in three blue-chip companies in Sri Lanka for more than 18 years from 1985. He became a Christian through Campus Crusade for Christ in

December 1988. Harry is married to Thisari, a physics and maths teacher, and they are blessed with two children, Sarah and Johaan. Harry graduated with an MBA in 2007 from the American International University in London. He also holds a BTh (Hons) from the University of Wales, Trinity Saint David, Lampeter, 2011. He is the founder and has been the pastor of the United Sri Lankan Christian Fellowship in Whyteleafe, Greater London, since 2008.

Bishop Dr Donnett Thomas was consecrated an Apostle in July 2003. She now provides an apostolic covering to three churches in Mombasa, Kenya, and one in Pradesh, India. She is also the senior pastor of Power of the Living Word Ministries International in Clapham Park, London. The ministry concentrates on teaching and equipping the Body of Christ, and she also fulfils her call to teach through her Institute for Life and regular church teachings. She was consecrated a bishop by the International Ministerial Council of Great Britain in November 2007. She has studied at the Institute of Christian Training (affiliated to the University of Wales) and has a BA Honours in Ministry from the Trinity Seminary and Theological College (affiliated to Canterbury University). She has an Honorary Doctor of Divinity from the Philadelphia Assemblies of Full Gospel Churches, awarded in 2000 in recognition of her excellence in teaching sound biblical doctrine. Apostle Donnett established the True Redemption Apostolic Network (TRANS) to identify and focus on teaching and equipping willing vessels anointed to carry the message of God to each generation, fulfilling the Great Commission and laying solid foundations in the lives of those ready to carry on the work in the kingdom of Heaven. Bishop Donnett Thomas has been married to Elder Colins for 41 years and they have two grown-up children.

Foreword

The importance of Christian mission can never be underestimated. It is central to any understanding of Christian discipleship. Its origins are found in the commissioning of the disciples by Jesus before his Ascension in the longer ending of St Matthew's Gospel, with the descent of the Holy Spirit on the Apostles at Pentecost and, of course, in the ministry of St Paul. The Acts of the Apostles describes in detail Paul's missionary journeys in which he sought out any opportunity to share the message of redemption that is freely given to anyone who accepts Jesus as Saviour.

The near 2,000 years since the ministry of St Paul contain many stories of missionary activity, including the work of those who from the mid-seventeenth century spread out across the world to take the Christian message, very much inspired by that injunction at the conclusion of St Matthew's Gospel, to:

> Go therefore and make disciples of all nations, baptising them in the name of the Father and of the Son and of the Holy Spirit, and teaching them to obey everything that I have commanded you. (Matthew 28:19–20)

The British mission agencies were very important in this process, and the stories of the sending of missionaries to far distant lands is an important part of church history. The names of many are lost in the passage of time, while a few are remembered as heroes of the faith whose endeavours are recognised and celebrated today.

The missionaries were all men and women of their time. They took their Christian faith, which was of course culturally defined, and while they brought great good, they often did so as part of a colonising mindset. In many cases, the countries to which they were despatched became part of the dominions of the English Crown and later the British Commonwealth. The ministry they offered was also in part a cultural imposition of British values that led many of those who came to faith to believe themselves to be part of a nation that was thousands of miles away, bound together in a great imperial family.

The history of how people from the colonies were received in the United Kingdom which accelerated as the Empire was dismantled following the Second World War is well documented. Many, to their astonishment and dismay, were made unwelcome in the churches they sought as home from home. Their experiences are documented in the essays that follow, in particular in the story of Philip Mohabir who, in the worst of times, was asked to leave the church where he had expected to find fellowship. By God's grace, Philip did not lose faith, and he became a pioneer of what the essays in this book explore.

Israel Olofinjana is to be congratulated for editing this book and for telling his own story of conversion to cross-cultural mission. In the Diocese of Southwark, where 35 per cent of our regular Anglican worshippers are black and Asian minority ethnic Christians, there is a strong awareness of global identity and cross-cultural interaction. The essays are compelling personal testimonies of 'reverse mission' – the ministry of disciples from around the globe who have responded to the call to bring the message and zeal for the gospel of those early missionaries back to the country from which it was sent.

The stories told in these essays are all personal and reflect the realities that had to be faced on arrival in the United Kingdom. Many worked with evangelical and Baptist churches as they took forward ministry and theological studies. There is deep wisdom in these pages which will contribute to current debates about missiology while drawing on experience of life and ministry.

José Carlos Lara from Brazil describes his ministry in Belfast during troubled times. His account of sharing in an ecumenical gathering and the aftermath of the family car being destroyed in an arson attack stands out as an example of speaking truth in divided communities. Donnett Thomas describes her early allegiance to the Black Power Movement in terms of somewhere to place her identity 'because that was not available in the church'. Jonathan Oloyede wrestled with the Lord, and the Lord won, with Jonathan turning away from a path that would have led to a successful medical career in Nigeria to accept the call of Christ.

The essays are in many ways about the necessity of truth being shared across divided Christian communities and finding expression in renewal within traditional churches as well as in the emergence and flourishing of black majority and Pentecostal churches. With the growing desire for unity in mission action between churches, evident in the commitment to ecumenical partnership, there is a recurring theme of strong hope for the future. The costly work of those who have struggled for change is beginning to bear fruit, notwithstanding the need for the structural changes, which Joel Edwards advocates if there is to be lasting transformation.

I commend the stories and testimonies in the pages that follow and pray that they will lead many to share the message of Jesus Christ in a world which may seem indifferent but where in reality there is a growing hunger and thirst for the gospel.

The Rt Rev Christopher Chessun
The Bishop of Southwark

Acknowledgements

There are a number of people who richly deserve thanks for their help and support in making this book a reality.

First and foremost are all the contributors who have graciously given their time and energy to reflect and write their stories. Thank you for all your efforts, for sharing so honestly and for responding to my requests and emails without complaint.

The idea for this book was first conceived in May 2012 when the Baptist Union of Great Britain's Assembly planning committee gave me the opportunity to organise a day conference on this subject. I want to thank the planning committee for this privilege of organising and leading the Turning the Tables on Mission conference.

One of the people who assisted me in organising that conference was Rev Carol Bostridge, who was also my colleague while I was serving as pastor at Crofton Park Baptist Church. Thank you for your help on the day, and for allowing me to serve as a colleague alongside you despite the fact that you were the senior pastor.

The congregation at Crofton Park Baptist Church deserve to be mentioned and thanked for welcoming me into their church family when I first arrived from Nigeria in 2004.

I am also indebted to the following people for their stimulating comments and insightful critique of the book manuscript in its early stages: Manoj Raithatha, National Coordinator of the South Asian Forum; Phyllis Thompson, Education Director of New Testament Church of God Leadership Training Centre; Rev Dr Steve Latham, Tutor at Spurgeon's College; Dr Andrew Rogers, Senior Lecturer at the University of Roehampton; Mark Sturge, Head of London Region, Christian Aid; Rev Joe Kapolyo, Senior Pastor of Edmonton Baptist Church and Dr William Ackah, Lecturer at Birkbeck, University of London.

Another person who deserves to be mentioned is Claire Siddaway of Latin Partners who opened my eyes to the immense contribution of Latin American missionaries in Britain. She went further to connect me with one of the Latin Link missionaries who has graciously contributed to this book.

I am grateful to all the people who have written a commendation for this book. This demonstrates that you believe in this project and the issues it is addressing.

Finally, I want to appreciate my wife, Lucy Olofinjana, who has always painstakingly and critically edited my books, including this one. Thank you for your patience and skill in ensuring that the books are readable and well presented.

Chapter One
Introduction
What is the meaning of 'Turning the tables on mission'?

Israel Olofinjana

What is meant by the phrase 'turning the tables on mission'? This phrase describes the concept of reverse mission: those from the former mission fields such as Africa, the Caribbean, Asia and South America sending missionaries and engaging in cross-cultural mission to the Western world. This implies a shift in the demographic centre of Christianity from the north to the global south. The papal election and appointment of the first non-European pope in the person of the Argentine Cardinal Jorge Mario Bergoglio (Francis I) in March 2013 illustrates this significant demographic change in world Christianity.

Philip Jenkins, in his book *The Next Christendom* (2007), acknowledged this geographical shift when he commented that 'over the last century ... the centre of gravity in the Christian world has shifted inexorably southward, to Africa and Latin America'.[1] The practical implication of this statement is that Africans, Asians and people from the Caribbean and South America are now sending missionaries to and planting churches in Europe and North America.

The BBC appears to have recognised this reverse flow of mission, as in early 2012 the television documentary *Reverse Missionaries* showed the efforts of three different short-term missionaries in Britain.[2] These missionaries were from Jamaica, Malawi and India, representing three continents from the global south.

---

[1] Jenkins, P. (2007), *The Next Christendom*, Oxford, Oxford University Press, p.1.
[2] *Reverse Missionaries*, a three-part documentary on BBC aired on 16th, 23rd and 30th March 2012.

Edinburgh 2010, an important world missionary conference, also symbolised the significance of this shift. Theologians, missionaries and practitioners from Africa, Asia and South America took the lead in presenting the majority of the papers used for discussion and reflection at the conference. The stakeholders of Edinburgh 2010 had committed themselves to appoint 60 per cent of the delegates from the global south in order to ensure that world Christianity was represented.[3] This marked a large shift, given that at the previous conference in 1910 the vast majority of the 1,000-plus delegates who attended were white males (from Britain and North America), with only a few delegates from India, China and Japan. Africans and South Americans were not represented at all.

Europe: the new mission field

Part of the rhetoric of reverse mission considers Europe as a mission field. This is due to the decline of Christianity and Christian values in the continent. A recent example of this decline in the United Kingdom is the 2011 census which showed a 13 per cent fall in those declaring Christianity as their religious identity – only 59 per cent compared to 72 per cent in 2001. While these figures only measure professed religious identity and not religious belief or practice, they are revealing, especially as there was also a ten per cent increase in those who profess no religion.[4] This means that British society is becoming an increasingly pluralistic secular society, religion apparently being systematically removed from the public square and discourse as the secular agenda grows.

The secular agenda began with the so-called 'Enlightenment' in the eighteenth century which asserted that humans were in charge rather than God. This, combined with the understanding that

---

[3] http://www.edinburgh2010.org/en/news/direct-mail/august-2009.html (accessed February 2012).

[4] http://www.ons.gov.uk/ons/rel/census/2011-census/key-statistics-for-local-authorities-in-england-and-wales/index.html (accessed December 2012).

evolution explained our origins, made it unnecessary for God to be a reference point any longer. The two world wars and the Holocaust also led to two fundamental questions being asked: the first, whether science and technology were really leading to progress; the second, whether there should be an absolute metanarrative that governed people's lives. The challenge of the first question led to people being cynical and sceptical about any agenda purporting progress, while the latter question caused people to doubt the existence of a supreme being. One result of not having an external absolute was the rise in loose morals such as marked the alternative sexual lifestyles and attitudes of the 1960s, which eventually led to a decline in Christian morality and values in our society.

In Britain we are now living in a postmodern, post-Christendom secular society which wants to confine faith to the private sphere, and any attempt to make it public is met with either opposition or discrimination. Evidence of discrimination against Christians seems to abound, with various discrimination cases faced by Christians at work, at school or in other public spaces. A report published by Premier Christian Radio in 2011 details the marginalisation of Christianity in British public life. The report states that:

> The general public agree a strong bias exists against Christians in British public life and that this is set to increase in the future.[5]

Further evidence is documented in a report by Christians in Parliament entitled *Clearing the Ground*. It states that:

> Christians in the UK face problems in living out their faith and these problems have been mostly caused and

---

[5] *Report on the Marginalisation of Christianity in British Public Life*, Evidence presented to the Clearing the Ground Parliamentary Inquiry into Religious Discrimination, Executive Summary, published by Premier Christian Media, 2007–2011.

exacerbated by social, cultural and legal changes over the past decade.[6]

Some commentators disagree, suggesting that there is not enough widespread evidence of systematic discrimination against Christians.

I would encourage caution that the term 'persecution' should not be used to describe what Christians are facing in the UK and would suggest that the words 'marginalisation' or 'discrimination' are more accurate. Persecution is what Christians are facing in places such as northern Nigeria, China, Egypt and Pakistan, where they confront being killed for their faith.

The global south: the new centre of the church

While European society is sceptical and cynical about faith and its adherents, Christianity is growing in Africa, Asia, South America and the Caribbean. For example, a church in Argentina has one of the largest Christian congregations in the world with more than 70,000 members.[7] This church, The Miracles of Jesus Renewed Christian Church (popularly known by the name of its radio broadcast Waves of Love and Peace), was founded in Buenos Aires by Hector Gimenez in 1983.

Another of the largest Christian congregations in the world can be found in South Korea. This is Yoido Full Gospel Church, founded by David Yonggi Cho (formerly Paul Yonggi Cho) in Seoul in 1958. At one time this church was the largest in the world, with approximately 750,000 members in the 1990s.[8]

---

[6] *Clearing the Ground Inquiry*: Preliminary Report into the Freedom of Christians in the UK, published by Christians in Parliament, 2012.

[7] Anderson, A. H. and Hollenweger, W. J. (eds) (1999), *Pentecostals After A Century*, Sheffield, Sheffield Academic Press, p.28.

[8] Wagner, Peter and Thompson, Joseph (eds) (2004), *Out of Africa*, California, CA, Regal Books, p.9.

Among the largest churches in Africa is Winners Chapel, founded in 1981 by the controversial Bishop David Oyedepo. This church made history in 1998 when Faith Tabernacle, their church auditorium, was dedicated. The auditorium can comfortably seat 50,000 people; it was at that time the largest church building in the world.[9]

So what are the factors that are causing explosive church growth in these continents of the global south? In the case of Africa, Christianity is growing in the midst of political dictatorships, political instability, economic recession, crippling inflation, extreme poverty, civil and tribal wars and high unemployment rates. While these hardships have encouraged many Africans to put their trust in God in order to survive, it must also be acknowledged that renewal (that is, experiencing God in a fresh way) is a major factor that is causing the growth of Christianity all over the continent. This renewal is mostly expressed through the Charismatic and Pentecostal churches in Africa, and it is these churches that are now taking the lead in planting churches in Britain and other European countries. In Britain, these churches are known as black majority churches (BMCs), and recent research conducted by Brierley consultancy indicates that these churches are among the fastest growing churches in London.[10] While this growth is attributed mainly to migration, it is still commendable. The history of BMCs in the UK can be traced back to 1906–1907 when the first African Pentecostal Church was founded in Peckham, south-east London.[11]

---

[9] Ojo, Matthew (2006), *The End-Time Army*, Trenton, NJ, Africa World Press Inc, p.166.

[10] http://www.brierleyconsultancy.com/images/londonchurches.pdf (accessed August 2013).

[11] http://israelolofinjana.wordpress.com/2012/05/06/the-first-african-pentecostal-church-in-europe-1906-present/ (accessed 15 August 2013). Adedibu, Babatunde (2012), *Coat of Many Colours*, UK, Wisdom Summit, p.26f. This church was Sumner Road Chapel and was founded by the late Rev Thomas Kwame Brem-Wilson c. 1906 in Peckham. The church is now known as Sureway International Christian Ministries and is based at Higgs Industrial Estate, Herne Hill.

Churches from the global south in Britain

BMCs are both independent and denominational churches that have emerged from the African and African-Caribbean diaspora communities. An example of an independent BMC is Kingsway International Christian Centre (KICC), founded in 1992 by Pastor Matthew Ashimolowo, while an example of a denominational BMC is the New Testament Church of God, founded in Britain in 1953 by the late Rev Oliver Lyseight. There are also BMCs that are part of the historic churches such as the Catholic Church, the Church of England, Baptists, Methodists and the United Reformed Church (URC). An example within the Baptist Union is Trinity Baptist Church in London, founded by Rev Kingsley Appiagyei in 1989.

Another development is the emergence of Latin or South American churches in Britain, of which one of the earliest is the Christian Community of London (CCL), founded by Pastor Edmundo Ravelo and his wife Asernia in 1985 after they came as missionaries to Britain in 1979. Another Latin American church is the Iglesia Misionera Evangélica led by the Peruvian missiologist, Rev Dr Samuel Cueva. This is a Spanish-speaking church that Dr Cueva planted in collaboration with St James Church, Muswell Hill in north London.

In addition, there are Asian churches such as Indian churches, South Korean churches, Chinese churches and Tamil churches, that have been founded in the UK. Possibly the first Asian church in Britain is the Chinese Church in London (CCiL) which was founded by Pastor Stephen Y T Wang in 1950. The church, now based in the Hammersmith area of London, is led by Pastor Siew Huat Ong who is the senior pastor.

The South Asian Forum (SAF) was established in 2010 under the umbrella of the Evangelical Alliance to support, encourage and equip South Asian Christians in their mission in the UK.[12] SAF was

---

[12] The countries in South Asia include India, Sri Lanka, Pakistan, Bangladesh, Nepal, Afghanistan, Bhutan and the Maldives.

also set up to represent the concerns of South Asian Christians to the government, society and the wider church.

Various factors such as exploration, commerce, the slave trade,[13] colonisation, imperialism and missionary intent led European missionary agencies to Africa, the Caribbean, Asia and South America. Similarly, different factors have caused the migration of Christians from the global south to the UK. These include economic recession, political insecurity (asylum seekers and refugees), educational opportunities and tourism. However in addition to these factors, people have also come as missionaries to plant churches and 'do' mission in Britain.

One such example is the late Guyanese Philip Mohabir who came as a missionary to England in 1956. What is interesting in Philip's story is that he was not sent by a church or mission organisation but by his Hindu family who were not fully aware of what he would be doing! His itinerant ministry led him to preach in various places in Brixton in shops and pubs, on the buses and from house to house.[14] He later planted churches and pioneered the founding of the West Indian Evangelical Alliance (WIEA) in 1984. WIEA was later known as the African and Caribbean Evangelical Alliance (ACEA) and has now been replaced by the National Church Leaders Forum (NCLF) and the One People Commission of the Evangelical Alliance.[15] A fuller story of Philip Mohabir is found in chapter ten of this book.

---

[13] While missionaries were not directly involved in the trading of slaves, they were involved indirectly through the wide acceptance of Hamitic Theology which asserts that black people were cursed and therefore inferior, giving reason for them to be enslaved. In addition, the Church of England profited through owning plantations in the Caribbean which used slaves for labour. Lastly, some missionaries had domestic slaves.

[14] Mohabir, Philip (1988), *Building Bridges*, London, Hodder and Stoughton, p.65.

[15] The National Church Leaders Forum (NCLF) had its first meeting at Kingsway International Christian Centre (KICC) in May 2011 and was attended by key leaders of the African and Caribbean churches in the UK. Its main purpose was to look at how African and Caribbean churches effectively serve their communities and the wider society, especially how it engages with political issues and policymakers. One People Commission

Another example of someone who came to the UK with missionary intent was Apostle Adejobi of the Church of the Lord Aladura in Nigeria. He came to Britain in 1961 to undertake a diploma in theology at the Glasgow Training Institute. After finishing his studies he came to London where he began a series of evangelistic meetings.[16] This eventually led to the founding of one of the first African Independent Churches (AIC) in Britain in 1964.

The 1980s witnessed African Pentecostal Churches sending pastors and missionaries to Britain to plant churches. Some of these church plants were focused on gathering scattered church members who resided in Britain. Examples of pastors sent to plant such churches include Matthew Ashimolowo, sent by Foursquare Gospel Church in Nigeria in 1984; Pre Ovia, sent by the Deeper Life Bible Church in Nigeria in 1985; and Titus David (deceased), sent by the New Covenant Church in Nigeria in 1986.[17] (In 1992, Matthew Ashimolowo left Foursquare Gospel Church to start an independent work – Kingsway International Christian Centre.)

The 1990s saw many missionaries being sent from South America to Europe. Latin American mission agencies were convinced that Europe was now the new mission field; therefore there was a need to send pastors and missionaries to preach the gospel. To this end, Latin Link, one of the major missionary agencies in South America, created Latin Partners in 1999 to be involved in the process of training and sending missionaries and pastors to Europe. They have since brought into Britain and Northern Ireland missionaries and pastors from Peru, Argentina and Brazil. One of these is Pastor José

---

started officially on 6th October 2011 as a body of the Evangelical Alliance made up of key national church leaders committed to celebrating ethnicity while promoting unity within the UK evangelical Church. Its vision is to see the UK church in all its vibrant ethnic diversity united as one.

[16] Sanneh, Lamin (1990), *West African Christianity*, New York, NY, Orbis books, p.204.

[17] Osgood, Hugh (2006), *African Neo-Pentecostal Churches and British Evangelicalism 1985–2005: Balancing Principles and Practicalities* (Unpublished PHD, School of Oriental and African Studies, University of London), pp 95-98.

Carlos Lara who is now working in Northern Ireland. His story is to be found in chapter three.

The year 2000 saw many more pastors and missionaries coming from the global south. A notable example was the invitation to Rev Joe Kapolyo from Zambia from All Nations Christian College in Hertfordshire to be its head. Joe Kapolyo responded to this call and became the Principal from 2001 until 2006. He is currently the Senior Pastor of Edmonton Baptist Church in north London.

My story

I came to the UK in 2004 as a missionary. I came to further my theological studies but I was also sent by my Pentecostal church in Nigeria to plant a congregation. I gave up this project after observing that there was a divide between the white and black churches in Britain and I decided to look for a white British church to fellowship with. I made this decision because I reasoned that if God had sent me to this country to do mission, I needed to understand the British context and also engage in cross-cultural missions rather than starting a Nigerian church.

A good place to start this journey was a British historic church, and for me this was Crofton Park Baptist Church in Brockley, south-east London. I was actively involved with youth work and other ministries within the church, and in 2007 I became a part-time minister there, working with Rev Carol Bostridge. In 2008 I became a full-time ordained and accredited Baptist minister, the first black minister in the 100-year history of Crofton Park Baptist Church. Carol and I had a fruitful ministry building on the multicultural layers of the church. For more of this story see chapter six.

The different stories in this book are all reflective of the various factors of migration such as economic recession, inflation, educational opportunities, political instability and, of course, ministry and missions.

New perspectives: Significant contributions of Christians from the global south in Britain

- The migration of Christians from the global south to the UK has led to new ways of doing church, with different forms and styles including African–Caribbean, African, Brazilian, South Korean, Chinese and Indian churches. While these types of church are not categorised as fresh expressions or emerging churches, they are definitely new and different ways of doing church in Britain.

- Christians from the global south are leading some of the largest churches or church gatherings in the UK. Kingsway International Christian Centre has about 12,000 people in attendance, and the Redeemed Christian Church of God's prayer gathering, Festival of Life, attracts about 40,000 participants twice a year. People in Britain are often very cynical about megachurches, questioning their effectiveness in discipleship and pastoral care. However, many of these churches have well-structured house groups that cater for the needs of people as well as discipling them. Megachurches are significant in an aggressive secular society that is trying to stamp out faith in the public square.

- Some of these churches are pioneering multicultural churches in the major cities in Britain. The term 'black majority churches' (BMC) does not mean that these churches are mono-ethnic or mono-cultural. The reverse is often the case because they may have people from different parts of Africa, different parts of the Caribbean and different parts of South America.

- These churches have brought fresh energy and passion through their various spiritualities such as New Year's Eve watchnight services, nights of prayer, united prayer and fasting, confidence in the Scriptures and Scripture meditation.

- These churches are contributing to global missions. In time past, global missionary enterprise appeared to be the monopoly of mission agencies and organisations from Europe and North America, but now BMCs are sending missionaries and church planters overseas. An example of a BMC sending missionaries overseas and engaging in church plants is Jubilee International Churches, founded by Dr Femi Olowo in 1992 in south-east London. Jubilee International Church has planted different church branches within Britain and other parts of the world, including Uganda, Kenya, Zambia, the Congo, Ghana, Ivory Coast, Sierra Leone and the Gambia, Pakistan, India and the Philippines. In addition, the church conducts mission trips to Europe, Africa and Asia. Some of the contributors in this book are involved in global missions. An example is Bishop Donnett Thomas who regularly travels to Zambia, Kenya and India for church planting purposes.

- The emergence and growth of these churches has led to new academic disciplines and modules in some British universities. I was privileged in 2011 and 2012 to help teach a course at the School of Oriental and African Studies (SOAS) on the subject of African Pentecostals in Britain. Joe Kapolyo, an African theologian and Baptist minister, observed that wherever Christians have crossed boundaries, this has led to new ways of reconceptualising the gospel, and this in turn has led to new university disciplines. European missionaries in Africa have led to academic disciplines such as social anthropology, tropical medicine and comparative linguistics.[18] Africans, Asians, South Americans and Caribbean people in Europe are paving the way for new studies such as New Religious Movements (NRM), immigration studies, empire studies, diaspora studies, African studies, Caribbean studies, post-colonial discourses and world or global Christianity.

---

[18] Kapolyo, Joe (2011), *Africans in the UK: Visible Christianity*, Mission Catalyst, issue 4, Baptist Missionary Society, p.3.

- Books and articles, academic and non-academic, PhDs and research projects are all being written on the phenomenon of the growth of these churches and their theologies. Philip Jenkins' book *The Next Christendom* (2001) is an example of Western scholarship showing interest in Christianity from the global south. I am also involved in a research project, Being Built Together, which is researching the history and church practices of BMCs in the London borough of Southwark. This project is jointly organised by Roehampton University, Churches Together in South London and Southwark for Jesus.[19]

The purpose of this book

Turning the tables on mission was the title of a Baptist day conference that I organised in May 2012, and which inspired the idea for this book and its title. At this conference, four speakers shared their inspirational journeys from the Caribbean, Africa and Latin America to Britain, where God has used them as ministers and missionaries. These four people were Rodrigo Assis da Silva, Joel Edwards, Dotha Blackwood and Jonathan Oloyede. I am extremely grateful that all four agreed to contribute to this book, enabling a wider audience to hear their wisdom and learn from their experiences.

The purpose of this book is fourfold. Firstly, it is to answer the critics of reverse mission. When I have had the privilege of speaking and presenting papers at conferences on the subject of reverse mission, one of the questions I am often asked is whether reverse mission is actually taking place; whether it is rhetoric or reality. The publication of my first book, *Reverse in Ministry and Missions: Africans in the Dark Continent of Europe* (2010), also prompted this question. We can understand the reasons for it, especially when we consider the fact that there are numerous cases of pastors from the

---

[19] http://www.roehampton.ac.uk/BeingBuiltTogether/Research/ (accessed 15 August 2013). This research project is now concluded and the findings of the research investigation were presented on 20th June 2013 at Southwark Cathedral.

global south leading churches which seem to only be made up of people from their own culture or ethnic background. However, that is not the entire picture as there are also cases of pastors from the global south engaging with people other than those from their own culture or ethnic background. The stories in this book serve as examples to demonstrate that reverse mission is a reality: the majority of the ministers and missionaries from the global south who are featured are engaged in cross-cultural mission and multicultural ministries in Britain and Northern Ireland. All have made the effort to not just remain among their own people, and this is also true for those who are leading ethnic minority congregations. This is an important point, as even when people are leading churches of their own ethnicity this does not mean that efforts have not been made to reach out cross-culturally.

Secondly, it is to allow reverse missionaries to tell their stories themselves. The stories in this book are told from a practitioner's point of view, allowing them to share their journey through autobiographical sketches rather than the analysis of an outsider. After all, people can tell their own stories better than anyone else, and this ensures that the stories are authentic. While this book will be more appealing to practitioners and those interested in the unfolding drama of reverse mission, it will also be of interest to scholars of the discourse of religion in the diaspora.

These autobiographies reveal details and nuances which help us to fully understand the phenomenon of reverse mission, and include details that challenge assumptions or stereotypes about migration from the global south to Britain. For example, as we read about what each individual was doing in their home country before coming to the UK, we realise that some have left lucrative jobs to answer God's call to Britain (for example, Rodrigo and Dotha). They are therefore not necessarily coming from a poor economic situation to enjoy a better material life in the UK. Another significant feature of these autobiographical sketches is that they give a holistic picture of people's cultural background and how this shapes their worldview and ministry in the UK context. This is important if we are to fully understand the narrative of reverse mission. For example, the spiritual worldview of Africans does not see a divide between sacred and secular spaces, therefore when African pastors and missionaries come to Britain they are often very bold about their faith in the public square.

The third purpose of this book is to create a resource for the church in the UK that can facilitate an understanding of Christians from other cultures. The influx of Christians from the global south in Britain warrants that UK Christians seek to understand Christianity from another culture or different theological background. I am afraid that this cannot be learnt through books written by Western scholars about Christians from the global south; it has to be heard from the people themselves. This is why, as detailed above, I have allowed each practitioner to write their own journey as a way to facilitate understanding for our British brothers and sisters. There is a lot to be learnt from us and about us, although much of the time I feel this is not communicated properly or from our own mouths. This book seeks to bridge that gap.

Lastly, this book is written with the hope that it will become a resource for not only our British brothers and sisters but also the many new arrivals of ministers and missionaries from the global south. The depth of experience on the mission field that is shared in this book should provide a mine of training resources for newcomers to the global north. In essence, it is written as a tool to equip those pastors and missionaries from the global south who often need training in cross-cultural mission. Bible colleges with a special interest in cross-cultural mission will also find this book a useful resource in equipping their students in global mission.

The stories that bring this book alive: chapter divisions

The chapters of this book are categorised under four major sections, representing the continents or regions that the writers have come from: South America, Africa, Asia and the Caribbean.

The South American section begins with the story of **Rodrigo da Silva** and is followed by that of **José Carlos Lara**. Both stories are twenty-first-century examples of missionary endeavours from South America and they signify the immense contributions of Brazilians to global missions. Rodrigo shares his story of leaving a lucrative job to come as a missionary from Brazil to Wales, later moving to Emmanuel Baptist Church in Thamesmead, London, where he became a youth leader, worship leader and assistant pastor.

José's story details his family's decision to answer God's call to serve among the ethnic minorities in Dungannon, Northern Ireland, despite the many setbacks and difficulties they faced. It also describes the realities of ministry in the context of the Catholic–Protestant tensions in Northern Ireland.

There are four contributors under the African section, starting with **Jonathan Oloyede**'s story. He shares his remarkable conversion from Islam to Christianity in Nigeria, and how on a three-month holiday to Britain in 1991 God specifically told him he had a mission to fulfil in the UK. He also describes his vision to see the different churches in the UK united in the place of prayer.

Jonathan's story is followed by my own missionary journey which started in 2004, and the stories of **Tayo Arikawe** and **Peter Oyugi**, both of whom also came to the UK in the 2000s. Tayo and Peter were both separately invited from their homelands to be part of the leadership team of independent evangelical churches in the UK. Before his call to Bristol, Tayo was faithfully pastoring a church in the Gambia. His ministry in Bristol is very fruitful and pioneering in terms of building a multicultural church and engaging in cross-cultural mission. Peter's story details his Christian Union background, training and development in Kenya. He also reflects on his call as an example of missionaries coming from the global south to the north, describing how he was invited directly from Kenya to pastor Elmfield Church in London.

There are two significant stories under the Asian section and both represent the stories of South Asians in Britain. **Ram Gidoomal**'s story is that of a first-generation South Asian in Britain. His story is particularly fascinating as he was born into a Hindu family, brought up in the Sikh faith and educated at a Muslim school in Kenya. Forced migration brought his family to the UK, and in 1971 he became a Christian. Deeply affected by the poverty he witnessed in India, he co-founded the Christmas Cracker project which mobilised people in the UK to raise money for the developing world in the

1980s and 1990s. This project was pivotal to the start of South Asian Concern (SAC) in 1989, and he describes the struggle and mission of South Asians in Britain and beyond.

Ram's story is followed by that of **Harry Tennakoon**, whose contribution takes into consideration his Buddhist background before he became a Christian. He also shares his journey of pastoring a Sinhalese speaking congregation in a largely Tamil church before he embarked on a separate church plant.

The final section tells the stories of people of Caribbean origins. Caribbean people are certainly the early pioneers of reverse missions in Britain, and Africans, South Americans and Asians today are all building on the labour of these early settlers and benefitting from their fruitful ministry. To illustrate this, the section starts with Caribbean pioneers and a tribute to the ministry and legacy of the late **Philip Mohabir**. His story is included because he is a true pioneer of reverse mission.

This is followed by a reflection from **Donnett Thomas**, Presiding Bishop of Power of the Living Word International Ministries and vice-chair of Churches Together in South London. Her brief contribution reflects on her background as a Jamaican growing up in Britain in the 1950s and also describes her current ministry. Bishop Donnett is an excellent example of a trailblazing woman who has greatly contributed to the Pentecostal and ecumenical scene in Britain.

The section continues with the story and reflections of **Dotha Blackwood** who shares her journey of being a reluctant missionary to Britain. Dotha left her banking job and ministry in Jamaica in order to come as a missionary to Britain in 1993. Her calling to the UK was confirmed with many testimonies of God's provision, and once here Dotha studied theology to Masters level in order to be able to train men and women for God's kingdom. She has lectured at Moorlands College and currently lectures at Spurgeon's College.

Finally, **Joel Edwards** reflects on the issue of identity and belonging for post-war Caribbean migrants arriving in Britain in the 1960s, who saw themselves as British citizens and were shocked to find that they were not welcomed as such. He traces the journey of black Christians in Britain from that of rejection to influence, adding that reverse missionaries in Britain must not just preach the gospel but affect social and structural change in Britain and other parts of the world as well. This is a thought-provoking point on which to end, and as someone who has seen and lived through the historical development of black majority churches in Britain, his conclusions are valid and significant. One salient point he makes is that a robust partnership is needed between those from the south and those from the north in order for reverse mission to fulfil its fullest potential and be a partnership that is neither patronising nor colonial.

SECTION A

SOUTH AMERICA

From Brazil to multicultural churches in Europe
Rev Rodrigo Assis da Silva

My journey in the kingdom:
a Brazilian missionary in Northern Ireland
José Carlos Lara

Chapter Two
From Brazil to multicultural churches in Europe:
Rev Rodrigo Assis da Silva

Christianity arriving in Brazil

Towards the end of the fifteenth century, the era of 'great navigations and exploration' started. Many European countries attempted to make long-distance sea journeys in order to find and exploit new lands and improve their trade profits. One of these nations was Portugal, which at that time enjoyed a super-power status as a nation in terms of trading, maritime technology and structure. The Catholic Church saw in these great navigations an opportunity to promote the gospel. So they offered Portugal a 'patronage agreement' which would allow the king of Portugal to establish and control new churches in the lands the Portuguese would 'discover'.

That is how Christianity arrived in my home country, Brazil. In 1500 AD, the first ships arrived in Brazil and the Portuguese took control of the coast. At first they exploited the forest, taking some of the finest wood, then they focused on gold extraction, and later they used the land for sugar plantations, constantly forcing Africans into slavery. Throughout this time of exploitation, the Catholic Church continued to send Jesuits to Brazil to catechise the indigenous people.

Later the Protestants arrived in Brazil, in 1555 AD with the French expeditions to Rio de Janeiro and in 1630 AD through Dutch expeditions to the state of Pernambuco. But it was only in the 1800s that Protestantism really started to gain considerable ground within Brazilian society, following the arrival of other Christian denominations such as the Presbyterians, Baptists and Methodists.

The religious atmosphere of the nineteenth and twentieth centuries in Brazil was marked by the development of a great rivalry between Catholics and Protestants (a term used to designate all non-Catholic Christian denominations collectively). In Pernambuco and the whole north eastern region of Brazil, these clashes between Catholics and Protestants often became hostile, to the extent that people were physically attacked and ridiculed socially because of their faith. It was in this region that my father was born.

Global northern missionaries reaching my family

My grandfather João Joaquim da Silva was born in Brazil in 1900. He was a successful farmer and business man in Caruaru, Pernambuco, owning several farms, a coffee factory and other small businesses. Some people in my family say his grandfather was Dutch; others say he was Portuguese. What appears to be certain is that he had rich European ancestors because my grandfather managed to accumulate such great wealth in a region that was considered to be the poorest and the least developed in Brazil. At that time, in Pernambuco people faced severe droughts, a general scarcity of water, improper sanitation, lack of employment and limited educational opportunities.

Although my grandfather was an influential person in the region, he was also caught up in the middle of the religious rivalry in Pernambuco. For a long time he was not a member of any church, but he always enjoyed engaging in respectful conversations about God with friends and pastors who would pass by his house. It was a Baptist missionary who, eventually, led my grandfather to make a commitment to Christ in 1947. Although we cannot be sure who the missionary was, we do know that my grandfather was baptised by David Mein, son of the British missionary John Mein.

John Mein was born in England in 1883 and moved to America to complete his ministerial training. He and his wife Elizabeth were appointed in 1914 as missionaries to Brazil by the International Mission Board (IMB).[20] In Brazil they planted churches, taught in a

---

[20] Formerly known as the Foreign Mission Board, the International Mission Board (IMB) is a missionary sending agency affiliated to the Southern Baptist Convention, based in Richmond, VA, United States. It currently has

seminary, founded schools and served in various capacities. Rev John Mein travelled a lot in the north east, preaching the gospel. His son, David, was born in 1919 in the USA during one of the family's ministry vacations. When David was ten he started following his father everywhere, playing a portable organ and supporting his father's missionary endeavours. Later in his life, David also felt called to the ministry; he spent a few years in the USA to train for ministry and returned to Brazil in 1944 as an IMB missionary.

Rev David Mein served as a missionary in Pernambuco for more than 30 years, pastoring a Baptist church, planting and giving support to churches in the countryside and teaching at the Baptist Theological Seminary. He was also one of the key leaders in the organisation of the joint public baptisms in the rivers of Pernambuco. At that time, this was never easy to organise, due to lack of water and opposition from Catholics.

In 1953, six years after his conversion, my grandfather travelled six hours on a horse to reach the river in Bonito, Pernambuco, where he was baptised. My father, Job Joaquim da Silva, who was seven years old, accompanied him. However, my father was not allowed to watch the baptism from close by because his clothes were dirty and he had sweat on them from the trip, so he hid behind the bushes. My father still remembers the scene of a very tall, white man with blonde hair baptising my grandfather and a crowd of people: the tall man was Rev David Mein.

I guess David Mein would never have imagined that one day there would be a shift in the direction of global missions, and that 55 years later, the grandson of someone he baptised in Brazil would come as a reverse missionary to England, his father's country of origin.

---

more than 5,500 missionaries serving in more than 130 countries around the world.

The Brazilian rural exodus

We hear different versions of exactly how my grandfather lost everything. Some people say he became a guarantor to a friend; others say he borrowed a large sum of money to invest in a new big business. Whichever story is true, something went wrong and my grandfather lost everything. He died one year later suffering from depression as he could not cope with the loss. After his death, my dad and his siblings found themselves in a very difficult situation. So my aunty Tete took the little money she had and bought a ticket to Sao Paulo, travelling three days by bus to get there.

Sao Paulo was thought to be a wonderful place to live during the 1960s and 70s because of industrial development. Millions of people were migrating to the state of Sao Paulo from different regions of Brazil. Aunty Tete went to Sao Paulo, found a job, made some money and paid the bus fare to bring the next sibling from Pernambuco. The next sibling came, found a job, made some money and sent money to bring the next sibling. And that was how, in a short period of time, my father and all his siblings (those who wanted to) migrated to Sao Paulo. The plan worked for them, but not for everyone. In a few years, Sao Paulo's economy was saturated and could not absorb everyone; in that process, many people ended up homeless, in poverty and living in slums.

When my dad arrived in the town of Santos, Sao Paulo, he found a job as a cleaner in a supermarket chain called 'Pão de Açúcar'. There he made his career for the next 35 years, slowly working his way up and reaching the post of section manager. My mother, Maria Eunice Assis da Silva, born in 1955, was an economics student who worked as cashier in the same supermarket. She was born and raised in Santos and her ancestors are difficult to trace, but just like my father's family, we do know that there were several inter-racial marriages between indigenous South American people, black Africans and white Europeans. In fact, the large majority of people in Brazil are the product of this racial mix. This racial mixture in my heritage was later very helpful in understanding and serving in multicultural churches.

The beginning of my passion for mission

My mother was brought up as a Pentecostal Christian. In 1910, two Swedish Baptist missionaries named Daniel Berg and Gunnar Vingren, influenced by the Pentecostal movement in America, left the Baptist church, went to Brazil and founded the Assemblies of God in 1918. My mother's grandparents were leaders in the Assemblies of God during its early stages, being also the fruit of the work of missionaries from the global north in Brazil. My mom was never completely satisfied in her church due to the strict rules they had to obey; therefore after my parents met in the supermarket and got married, they started going to a Baptist church together, and were later ordained as deacons.

I was born in 1981 and, together with my brothers Helder and Andre, I was brought up in the ways of the Lord, and have been quite involved in church since I was a young boy. I really understood the message of the gospel when my Sunday school teacher explained the importance of a personal commitment to Christ. I accepted Jesus as my Saviour and Lord and was baptised before I was a teenager. Around that time, I started to develop an admiration for the ministry, especially mission. I was fascinated to see pastors coming from different nations to preach in my church or do missionary work in my town. I would sit in the front row in church when they were preaching; I would follow them everywhere they went. I would constantly annoy them as I tried to practise the few words of English I thought I could pronounce.

Throughout my childhood, we always led a simple life. My parents could not afford to pay the fees for a private English school, which is the best way to learn English in Brazil. Therefore, when I was 14, I asked my father to allow me to work so that I could pay for English classes. But he wanted me to concentrate on my normal studies, so we had numerous arguments about that. When he realised that there was no way to stop me, he offered me a job in the supermarket where he worked. My job was to put people's shopping in the bags and take it to their cars or houses. With my first salary I went to that private English school and enrolled myself on the course. I had no idea of the massive impact this would have on my future ministry.

Life was pretty busy for me as a teenager: I would go to school Monday to Friday from 7am to 1pm and then work in the supermarket Monday to Saturday from 2pm to 8pm. My English class was every Saturday from 9am to noon and I had homework to do almost every evening. Obviously, Sunday was the best day of the week for me. I was still very much involved in church, doing drama, playing musical instruments in the worship team and taking part in the youth group's activities. School holidays were also a great time, as there were always missionaries coming from the US or the UK. I was now able to communicate better with them and was even able to interpret for them in different churches. This was how I met a pastor from the US called Mark Troncale, who was one of the first people to recognise my calling to ministry. I was 17 at this time. Mark encouraged me to pray more seriously about it. I also met Gary Plumley from Wales.

My calling and training for ministry

Gary came to Brazil with the intention of starting a missionary youth exchange project. I was 18 when I met him and was one of the first young people to be invited to serve voluntarily in Wales for one year. However, in that same year I had taken an exam to join the Brazilian Air Force and was accepted. This was a great opportunity for me to have a stable and well-paid job – something that is quite rare in Brazil. I had a decision to make and did not know what to do. I remember that around that time some friends from the church passed by my house for my birthday, including the pastor, who shared this Scripture with me: '"For I know the plans I have for you," declares the Lord, "plans to prosper you and not to harm you, plans to give you hope and future"' (Jeremiah 29:11).

God had a plan, and all I had to do was to find out what exactly He wanted from me. As I kept praying and discussing the possibilities with my parents, pastors and friends, God made it clear that He wanted me to take the job in the Air Force and stay in Brazil.

I obeyed and stayed in Brazil. I was not in a very high rank (I was an airman working in administration), but it was a great experience and the salary was also very good for a 19-year-old boy. Soon I bought my own motorcycle and my professional prospects were very good.

In my second year of working for the Brazilian Air Force, I was selected to undertake a special training course in helicopter mechanics. This would increase my professional prospects even more. After two months on that course, although I was happy, something was still bothering me. I could not stop wondering whether God was calling me to ministry instead. Somehow, I knew that the longer I stayed in the job, the more difficult it would be to leave it. Moreover, legally I could not leave the job at any time: I had one chance every two years to decide whether or not I wanted to renew the contract for another two years. At this stage the time for renewal was approaching.

I spoke to my pastor about my thoughts and feelings and we started praying. I was 21 years old by then. After a few months I came to the conclusion that I should stay in my job but also prepare to serve God at the same time. I decided to stop the course in helicopter mechanics and instead started theological training at the Baptist College. However, I did not leave my job completely. My plan was to continue to work in the Air Force, using my salary to pay for my theological training, and with time figure out what God wanted me to do.

I started my theological training in August 2002. Every weekday I had to go to work during the day, then in the evening I would travel 120km to the Baptist College in Sao Paulo where I had classes from 7pm to 10pm. After that, I had to travel back to my home town, another 120km. This was very tiring; I was sleeping an average of five hours every night. After two years of doing that, I was exhausted. I eventually realised it was impossible to keep doing both. I had to give up something – either my theological training or my career in the Air Force. I started seeking God's direction once again. This was a life-changing decision, and the time for my second contract renewal was approaching.

I sought to understand God's will through prayer, His Word and also talking to my pastors about their own calling into ministry. It became clear to me that God wanted me to leave my job in the Air Force to dedicate myself solely to my theological training and to serve Him in full-time ministry. That conviction came to my heart as I reflected on my life experience and understood the progressive way in which He had been calling me to ministry. This had begun when I was a child, through that inexplicable admiration for missionaries that He had put in my heart, and it was now culminating in this strong conviction and willingness to give up everything to serve Him. This does not mean that I was not afraid: it was not easy to exchange a stable professional career for an unknown and uncertain future. Some people said I was crazy for doing it. But my parents and brothers gave me their full support.

Following that decision, I felt led by the Lord to speak to the pastor of a church near the Bible College in Sao Paulo. This was the first time I had met Pastor Joao Marcos Barreto Soares. I went to talk to him and explained my situation. Surprisingly, by the end of our first conversation, he offered me full support, accommodation in the church manse, payment of my college fees by the church, his mentorship and the possibility of doing my ministry placement in his church (something that the Baptist College requires all students to do from the third year)! The way that God opened the doors for me through Pastor Joao was another confirmation that I was on the right path, and the enormous impact of his life on my ministry would become obvious in the following years.

The beginning of my ministry: Brazil, Mozambique and Wales

Now I was free to dedicate myself to study and to serve God almost full-time. I still had to give some private lessons (helping children with homework) to earn some money, but most of the time I was free to do what I felt called to do – to practise what I was learning at the Bible College in different areas of the church, including: children's work, youth ministry, worship team, Bible teaching and evangelism. I did this in Brazil for the following two and a half years while completing my theological studies. When I finished my studies in December 2006, under Pastor Joao's guidance, the church gave me the opportunity of a mission trip to Mozambique as an 'end of course gift'. I was expected to support Pastor Sergio de Olivera, a Brazilian missionary to Mozambique, in organising evangelistic events and in offering some training to the church leaders, musicians and youth leaders of the churches he led in Maputo.

I was in Mozambique between December 2006 and February 2007 and had an incredible time. The fact that they have a similar climate to Brazil and the same language helped a lot, but that did not make me immune to the culture shock. It was the first time I had been immersed in another culture and experienced a completely different way of living and believing. I was amazed to see the way people enthusiastically sang and danced to the Lord during the services. I was struck by the stories of miracles and the accounts of spiritual battles against the occult. Moreover, my theoretical concepts of mission were confronted daily by the pragmatic challenges of mission. In one case, for instance, there were some polygamist women who accepted Christ, and Pastor Sergio had to decide whether to consider it as sin and tell those women to abandon their husbands (and thus condemn them to a life of poverty and marginalisation), or find a different way of dealing with the situation that would be more accepting of polygamy as a normal aspect of their culture. That kind of situation made me realise that the work of a missionary can be much more complicated than I had previously thought.

When I was in Mozambique, I would often write to Gary – the Welshman who had invited me to come as a missionary to Wales seven years before. I shared with him a little of what I was doing in Mozambique, and in response he invited me once again to come to Wales. Somehow I felt that this could be the right time, and we agreed to discuss it further when I was back in Brazil. However, when I arrived in Brazil, Pastor Joao also had some news to share: his associate pastor was leaving and he wanted me to stay and work with him.

Take note that, in Brazil, I would have had a quite well-paid position in a very renowned church in Sao Paulo. Moreover, I would have been working in my own country, close to my family, with people I already knew, under the guidance of a senior pastor who was my friend and from whom I could learn a lot. In Wales I would work voluntarily, I had to pay for my flight, and they would only give me food and accommodation once I was there. Moreover, I would be far from my family and had no idea what to expect in terms of the church and people. Pastor Joao, Gary and I prayed for a while and it became clear that God wanted me in Wales.

Something else very special happened during my short stay in Brazil, between my mission trip to Mozambique and my year in Wales. It was in March 2007 that I first met Annalena, who would later become my wife. She was a German social work student who came to Brazil to visit some friends and learn about a Christian social project in Sao Paulo. We had a mutual friend and got to know each other through him. The social project she wanted to visit was led by another friend of mine from the Bible School, so I took her to see it. We talked a lot and became friends, and the rest is history as we are now happily married.

I came to serve voluntarily as a missionary in the Welsh valleys in July 2007 and stayed there for a year supporting the work of two different churches in Abertridwr. One was a Welsh Baptist church and the other was an independent community church. I was part of a team of three Brazilian missionaries helping with evangelism, youth work, preaching and teaching, worship and music, the senior citizens group, visitation and other ministries.

To be honest, I struggled a little in the beginning because I came from a context in which a lot of young people fight for any opportunity in life, and it was therefore quite shocking for me to see the large numbers of young people who were wasting their lives in Wales either by getting drunk every evening or dropping out of school for no reason. It was also difficult to adapt to the fact that the people in general are more reserved than they are in Brazil. In addition, the great difference in the climate and the fact that I had difficulty understanding the Welsh accent at the beginning played a part in my frustration. Notwithstanding, the people from the village were very affectionate in their own way and really enjoyed getting to know us and talking to us. The fact that as a team of three missionaries we were very supportive of each other also helped me a lot.

When I came, I knew that there were differences in the way European people believed and expressed their faith, but knowing something is not the same as experiencing it first hand. In Brazil, it is not normal for Christians to drink alcohol or for a young, non-married Christian couple to be chatting alone in a room. In Wales, both of these things were completely normal. In Wales I also had to call people and ask for permission before visiting them. I could not just show up on their doorstep as I would normally do in Brazil. I could mention several things, but the main culture shock for me was in relation to the way people talked about problems or discussed strategies in church. I have observed that in Wales, and in Britain in general, expressing your views and offering constructive criticism is often seen as confrontational, whereas in Brazil this is not the case. This led to a few problems and misunderstandings for me.

After a while, I realised that in most cases there is not necessarily a right or a wrong way of practising your faith. Of course, that which is intrinsically sinful must be challenged, but in the majority of cases it is simply a cultural issue and it is totally normal that people relate to God and read the world through the lenses of their culture. Once we focus on what we all have in common (our love for the Lord), we can develop a respectful, positive attitude towards each other. Loving others as we love God and pulling together in the same direction as a church regardless of our cultural differences are very important. As a missionary in Wales, I not only had to adapt my worldview and learn how to do things differently, but I also had to find ways to encourage indigenous Welsh, and later English, Christians to do the same in relation to us.

Serving in a multicultural church in Thamesmead, London

By the end of my time in Wales, I had heard about a very interesting MA course in Religious Education at King's College London. I applied for the course and was offered a place. I then contacted the London Baptist Association (LBA) saying that I would like to work for a church in London on a part-time basis while completing my course. They circulated my information to several Baptist churches in London, and in that same week I received emails from about five different churches inviting me for an interview. I was very surprised, but that opened my eyes to the fact that there is a great need for church workers like me in Britain. Emmanuel Baptist Church in Thamesmead (EBCT) was one of the churches that contacted me, and their faith led them to invite me to work with them without having even met with me personally, as I was in Brazil for a couple of months to sort out the necessary documentation.

I changed my volunteer work visa for a student visa and on 15th September 2008 I arrived back in London. In the first year, I completed my MA course and worked part-time at Emmanuel Baptist Church, mainly in the youth ministry. In my second year, after finishing my course, I started serving as an assistant pastor with specific responsibilities for the youth, young adults, worship team, training & discipleship and mission & evangelism ministries. I can say to the honour and glory of God that He gave me a lot of wisdom and strength throughout my ministry at Thamesmead so that the church experienced significant growth and development in all the areas of ministry that I was overseeing.

We established a strong and consistent programme for the young people which included Bible classes on Sunday mornings, youth meetings on Friday evenings, an annual summer youth trip and a Saturday monthly social/outreach event. The latter had about 70 teenagers in attendance between the ages of 11 to 18, from both our church and the local community. Several of these young people ended up coming to the Friday youth devotional meetings. The young adults' ministry (ages 19 to 29), which was non-existent when I first arrived, was established and is now enjoying similar activities as those offered to the young people, but specifically for that age group.

There were also several changes to the worship team, which became more inclusive of teenagers who were gifted singers and musicians. In addition, the church became stronger in evangelism and community work through several initiatives and projects we developed such as concerts, international evenings, children's holiday clubs, school assemblies, hosting missionaries from abroad, football matches and so on. But probably the most important contribution of my ministry at Thamesmead was the establishment of a successful all-age Bible School on Sunday mornings before the service.

None of the above things were easy to implement, as they never are for any pastor in any kind of church. However, at Thamesmead I was faced with an interesting challenge that I had not encountered before. Even though I had been trained for the ministry and had some ministry experience (part of which included cross-cultural mission), I had never served in a multicultural church before. This made my ministry at Thamesmead much more challenging, but also very interesting and enriching.

I will now share some of my experiences as a mixed-race Brazilian reverse missionary serving in a multicultural church at Thamesmead, London. I have no intention of approaching this topic from an academic perspective, nor is it my desire to assume an authoritative position on the subject, offering answers as if I am an expert. I will simply relate some stories, describing some of the challenges I faced, the way I dealt with some of the issues and even some of the mistakes that I made. I hope that the reflections I offer here about my journey into multicultural ministry will be beneficial to others who already are, or are willing to be, involved in multicultural churches, and that they will bring some encouragement and insight.

Multicultural ministry and church racial categorisations

It was in London that, for the first time in my life, I was confronted with the fact that churches can be categorised along racial lines. Examples are white British churches, black majority churches, Hispanic or Latin American churches, 'ethnic' churches, multicultural churches or other terms related to race. This basically does not exist in Brazil. There you will find a different type of church division based on people's socio-economic conditions rather than race. So when I first came to London, it was strange for me to constantly hear racial terms being attributed to churches in almost every conversation about church and Christianity.

The church I came to serve at Thamesmead had made a long transition from being a white British church to becoming a multicultural church with the motto, 'a house of prayer for all nations'. The majority of the congregation was black African and Caribbean, but there were also white British people, Asians, people from other European countries and some Hispanic people as well. My first questions were, why had the majority of the white British people left? And what did the church mean by claiming to be a multicultural church, when it was labelled as a black majority church by others?

I found the answer to the first question by talking to other people and reading the history of the church. I discovered that the white British members had left mainly because they were no longer comfortable in the church as people from other cultural backgrounds joined. I also later found out that this was very common in churches transitioning into multicultural congregations. This is sad, as I think a major concern of any truly multicultural church should be to keep members from the dominant racial group as they add members from different racial groups. How exactly that is possible I do not know, but surely it will require a lot of love and flexibility from all involved. It will also require a leadership that brings people together and helps the different groups to understand and respect each other as they celebrate diversity and unity in Christ.

The answer to the second question was obvious: the church in Thamesmead was labelled a black majority church because the majority of the members of the congregation had an African or Caribbean background. I had to come to terms with the fact that it was normal to categorise churches that way in England, even though that was not normal for me and the term sounded quite rude and prejudiced to my ears.

Reading books written by observers and practitioners of multicultural ministry helped me to further answer my questions. A multicultural church is commonly defined as one in which there are several nations represented and where the dominant nation does not make up more than 80 per cent of the congregation. Even though the congregation at Thamesmead was composed of about 80 per cent black people, they all came from several different countries in Africa and the Caribbean. Even those who came from the same nation were often from different tribes and spoke different languages. Take Nigerians, for instance, who composed the largest group in the congregation (60 per cent, perhaps): there were Hausas, Ibos, Yorubas and several other minor tribes represented – each one holding their own unique language and culture. It was a similar story with the Ghanaians, and others. Therefore the church in Thamesmead was truly a multicultural church, even though this would not be immediately obvious to an outsider because of the other more evident label the church had: a black majority church.

I was amazed by what I had encountered in Thamesmead in particular and in England in general. Impressed by the influence of issues of race and identity in relation to the dynamics of a church, I embedded myself in this new context. I was forced to reflect on my own race and several other aspects of my identity. I remember being very surprised when a group of people from church first referred to me as a 'mixed-race guy'. Even though it was true, strangely, no one had ever applied that term to me before, nor had I ever heard it applied to another person. In Brazil, people did not bother about the colour of my skin; in Mozambique I was seen as a white guy; in Wales and Germany, people see me more as a black person. So, being called 'mixed-race' was a new thing for me. My main question at that time was, how would their perception of me as a mixed-race Brazilian guy help or hinder my ministry in this multicultural community? To start, one has to be aware of the influence and perception of his own identity in order to minister in a multicultural setting.

In my first conversation with Rev Pat Took, the former team leader of the London Baptist Association, she commented that she really believed that because of our inherently mixed cultural background, Brazilian ministers had an advantage in bringing people together and avoiding potential conflicts in multicultural churches. That is why she had encouraged the church in Thamesmead to take the opportunity to invite me to work with them. I did not have time to explore the reasons why she had that conviction, but those words, coming from someone of such wisdom and experience, really got me thinking about the purpose of God in bringing me to serve at Thamesmead. Was I someone like Esther, put by God in Thamesmead 'for such a time as this' (Esther 4:14)?

Multicultural ministry and racial representation in leadership

One of the first problems I identified as soon as I arrived at Emmanuel Baptist Church in Thamesmead was that, even though they were a truly multicultural church, the leadership team did not represent the make-up of the church very well. Out of 15 people in the leadership, eight were white British. As an assistant pastor, my scope of action was limited and it was not my responsibility to change that. Notwithstanding, I tried to influence people from different backgrounds to accept nominations to join the leadership team in order to make it more representative of the congregation's make-up. I am glad to say that things were more balanced after four years.

However, the more that people from different backgrounds joined the leadership team, the more difficult it became to discuss topics and reach decisions at leadership meetings. My observation was that some of the white British leaders expected the leadership meetings to be fairly logical: presentation of the topics, discussion and decisions. Some of the ethnic minority leaders, however, expected it to be more spiritual, with topics being soaked in hours of prayer before a decision could be reached. When the discussion actually started, some of the white British leaders were very concise, assertive and, sadly, sometimes even imposing and disdainful in their comments. In exchange, the majority of the black African leaders were never completely frank and open about their disagreements, often choosing instead to tell a long story in the meeting, hoping that others would be able to guess what their opinion was through that story.

As a mixed-race Brazilian, I had the advantage of being in a neutral position in the leadership group. My experience of serving in Wales and my international marriage to a German white lady had helped me to become acquainted with a different way of thinking and perceiving the world. The white British people in church really respected the fact that I had spent time in Wales before coming to London. My time serving in Africa and the influence of African culture in Brazil also helped me to understand another way of reasoning and making sense of the world. Even though Africa is a big continent and their cultures and lifestyles are so different, the fact that I had previously served there enabled the black people in the church to empathise with me and also to believe that I could actually understand where they were coming from.

Working with a leadership team that represents the church's racial make-up is not a small challenge, but I believe that it is the right thing to do. However, it has to be done in a way that reflects God's kingdom and not only to appear to be inclusive and 'politically correct'. It has to be done with the sincere intention of taking on board people's opinions and with a willingness to learn from each other, believing that it is possible to share power and discern together the will of God for the church. As I tried to positively influence this multicultural leadership team, I realised that my leadership style and my attitude towards others as a pastor was the pivotal factor in the process of bringing leaders together. As a pastor, I could not always understand where others were coming from, but people were satisfied if I was seen to be making a sincere effort. Above all things, they would be happy if their opinions as individuals were valued and respected. Patronising comments, sarcastic responses and disrespectful behaviour would leave them very upset.

Multicultural ministry and conflict management

Several times while serving the church at Thamesmead, I found myself being the bridge in communication. Much of who I am and what I have experienced in life started to make sense to me as I began to assume that position of mediation. A big part of this process of building bridges involved trying to help people from different backgrounds to listen to each other first and then to attempt to understand where each other was coming from.

There was a tense moment in the life of the church when the white British people were very upset with the black people because they were always late. Things became even worse when a group of black Nigerians and Ghanaians proposed that the church should offer Bible classes before the main service on Sundays. 'You people are never here in time for the service. Do you really want us to believe you will come one hour before the service for Bible classes?' was one of the answers they received. This led to a conflict that could easily have split the church.

In managing the situation, I tried to explain to people from other backgrounds that Bible classes on Sundays is a big part of what it means 'to be church' for West Africans. I also had to tell the group of Nigerians and Ghanaians that the others had a point as they were indeed always late, and that was not going to work in their favour. In response, the West Africans argued: 'The sheep goes where there is pasture. We do not think we have been spiritually fed here. That is the main reason why people do not really bother coming on time.'

That discussion went on for a few weeks and I remembered something that Pastor Joao had once told me in Brazil:

> When people come to you with suggestions about church, if it is not something absurd and sinful, it is always preferable to allow them to go along and do what they think God is telling them to do. If it is from God, it will be a success, and you will not be a hindrance. If it is not from God, it will die quickly, and no one will have cause to accuse you of being a controlling pastor and a hindrance.

With that in mind, and as a way to resolve the issue, I proposed a six-month trial period for the Bible school. I must confess that I thought it was not going to work, even though quite a few people had enrolled and seemed to be very excited about this new ministry. I gathered a group of more experienced Christians from within the congregation and prepared them to teach alongside me. I also took responsibility for advertising the courses and preparing the lessons every week.

I was surprised when in our first session in 2010, I saw a crowd of people in church one hour before the normal time of the service, ready to study the Word of God. For the first weeks an average of 70 per cent of the congregation attended different Bible classes. I thought the numbers would decrease with time, but on the contrary, more and more people started coming, and what started as a trial period to avoid a possible conflict became one of the main ministries of the church. The Bible school also helped us to become a stronger intergenerational church, as having classes for different ages before the service meant that the young people (11 to 18) did not have to go out to their classes in the middle of the service as before, so they stayed in the service and got involved in several ministries.

There were several other tense moments in the life of the church that were simply caused by the multicultural nature of the congregation. There was one occasion in which a white British preacher speaking on Palm Sunday decided to invite one of our teenagers to be the donkey on which Jesus entered Jerusalem. The young boy, who happened to be from Nigeria, had to crawl to the front of the church pretending to be a donkey as a sermon illustration. The Nigerians in the church were furious after the service as they found this very insulting. On another occasion, a person from an ethnic minority background was angered because someone was nodding as he was speaking in the church meeting, and apparently this was something very offensive in his culture.

These types of conflicts are not insignificant challenges. First, they require a lot of dedication and humility from all concerned in order to make an effort to listen and try to understand where each other is coming from. This helps to establish what is meant and how both parties feel about what has happened. Second, they require a lot of flexibility and wisdom so that people can move past what has happened and continue to pull together in the same direction, regardless of their differences, focusing on Christ. This is all impossible without forgiveness, where those who were offended acknowledge that, in the majority of the cases, the other had no intention to offend, and the one who caused offence apologises.

The active involvement of the pastor in leading these reconciliation processes and dealing with potential conflicts is crucial. As small and unimportant as they may seem, no situation that involves a cultural or racial aspect should be overlooked in a multicultural church. A small tension, if not resolved, can easily develop into a serious conflict that grows out of proportion. Such situations have the potential to affect more people in church than those initially involved, as others take sides simply in order to 'stand for their own people'.

Multicultural ministry and the way we address people

The multicultural characteristic of the church in Thamesmead forced me to also reflect on another aspect of my own identity and the way it could enhance or hinder my ministry. This had to do with power issues surrounding names, titles and the way we address people and allow them to address us in church. As I arrived in Thamesmead, I had to give up my real name ('Rodrigo', with a strong 'R' at the beginning that sounds like 'H'), as almost no one could pronounce it properly. The majority of the white people in the church simply called me by what became my first name – Rod. The majority of the older black African and Caribbean folks would call me Pastor, Sir, or even Reverend. However, the black African and Caribbean young people tended to call me by my first name, and were often rebuked and told off by the older black folks who would label the youngsters as being disrespectful to the pastor.

I simply took the approach of not imposing my own way and allowed every individual to use whatever term they thought was appropriate, be it Pastor, Reverend, Rod or Uncle. This I had also learnt from Pastor Joao in Brazil, as we have a similar tension in churches over there with some people calling the pastor by their first name and others calling them Pastor.

In addition, I tried to be respectful and culturally sensitive by using the appropriate terms towards other people in the church. For instance, I would call some of the elderly African and Caribbean people uncle or aunty, and some of the elderly white folks Mrs and Mr, unless, of course, they said I should call them by their first name or by the usual church terms 'brother' and 'sister'.

I had learnt that as a pastor of a multicultural church, I had to be flexible, approachable and culturally sensitive with these issues of addressing people. But I soon also learnt that I could run into all sorts of difficulties where there were power issues at stake. There was a situation when a black African elderly man, whom I addressed as 'uncle', requested me to call him 'prince', because that was the title he had inherited as part of a tribal royal family in Africa. There was also a situation in which people who had been elected as deacons and lay pastors were drawing too much attention to their new titles.

In cases like these, I always felt it was my duty to highlight that we are all equal in the sight of the Lord. I did this through polite but firm personal conversations with some people. I also did it through my general teachings in church, in which I would often include an explanation of the biblical meaning of the words 'minister' and 'deacon' as functions rather than titles.

There were also other trickier cases around the issue of addressing people in church. These cases did not particularly involve power struggles, but another problem: cultural projections. There was an occasion, for instance, when a Pakistani lady was giving a children's talk in church and taught all the children, regardless of their cultural background, to call every older person in church 'uncle' or 'aunty'. This, according to her, was the respectful way of addressing older people and the way to please God. Some people in church applauded her; others were not so happy that she was imposing and projecting her own cultural values on the children.

Different kinds of cultural projections happen very often in a multicultural church, and I believe it is the task of the pastor to remind people with gentleness that not everything in their culture can be taken as scriptural in the life of the church. It should not be imposed on others as the only and truthful way.

Multicultural ministry and reaffirming cultural identity

As I observed the way people addressed me, I noticed that some Asian children would always refer to me as uncle when they were close to their parents. However, when their parents were not near, they would call me by my first name. It was then that I realised that, just like me, the majority of the young people (and several young adults and adults) in this multicultural church were also wrestling to make sense of their own identities as individuals who belonged to an ethnic minority group but were also living in London and immersed in the British culture.

I thought it was part of my task and responsibility as a pastor to help them deal with those identity issues as I also tried to deal with these issues myself. This task involved some biblical teaching – for instance, discussing the stories of Daniel in Babylon, Joseph in Egypt or the parable of the Good Samaritan and comparing the racial and cultural issues of those stories to our present times and applying biblical principles to our challenges today.

This task, however, required more than biblical teaching. I noticed that it was also important to reaffirm people's cultural identities in more pragmatic ways, valuing and teaching them to value their culture of origin, and at the same time helping them to be and feel more included within the British society. I did encourage some people in church, including some Latinos, to take English classes and become more involved with festivals and other more British activities that were going on in our community. I started using PowerPoint presentations in my sermons to help them understand the message and improve their English skills. We celebrated and discussed the meaning of the British holidays and special dates in church.

At the same time, I also encouraged some African teenagers to visit their home countries with their parents. I told people to be proud that they were able to speak a different language, and would encourage the teenagers to keep practising their mother tongue and suggest to the young adults that they include their mother tongue as an ability in their CVs and job applications.

I also told people to be proud of the English that they could speak. When, for instance, church members came to me saying they would not get involved in teaching the children because they knew people would laugh about their accent. I would tell them, 'I am a stranger, I have an accent, and I preach. People sometimes laugh at me, but I don't mind; I am doing the will of God. Why can't you do the same?'

The other way we encouraged people in reaffirming their cultural identities was through the establishment of international activities, such as our international evenings. This was an annual event in which church members were invited to come along, share typical national dishes and give a presentation on their country of origin (by singing, dancing, speaking or any other means). This should be one of the highlights of any multicultural church as it gives people an opportunity to demonstrate a visible aspect of their own cultural identities while observing and learning more from other cultures.

A bolder step that I took towards the end of my ministry at Thamesmead was the introduction of multilingual worship. The church was already used to worshipping God through the use of different rhythms and styles, including African and Caribbean beats. But how happy, valued and reassured people felt when, in our Sunday services, we started using the chorus of very well-known songs translated into their mother tongues. For instance, we would sing: 'Holy, Holy, Holy; I want to see you.' Then we would repeat the same line in Spanish: 'Santo, Santo, Santo; Yo quiero verte'; and then in Korean: 'Korug, Korug, Korug; Chubogehasoseo'. On another Sunday we would sing the song 'God is so good, is so good to me', repeating the chorus in Yoruba: 'Oluwa dara, O dara funmi'; and then in Ga (a kwa language spoken in Ghana): 'Mi Nyomo Hi, Nyomo hi hami'.

We did the same with different songs, using several languages and dialects that were represented in the church. I would ask people to translate the chorus, which was also a part of the process of reaffirming their cultural identities. The introduction of multilingual worship did not take too much of our normal worship time on Sunday. It was only one chorus of one song (perhaps translated into three languages other than English). Out of eight complete songs we would normally sing this was very little, but it was just enough to reaffirm the cultural diversity of the church without making it boring and off-putting for others who had no ability or interest in learning other languages.

As in any other setting and context, in a multicultural church it will always be impossible to make everyone happy. In one case, a Hispanic lady in church was upset because the leaders did not organise a watchnight service on Maundy Thursday as she was used to in her tradition. In other words, she thought we failed to reaffirm and value her Christian cultural identity. She did not realise that we had tried it before and it had not worked very well. She also did not realise that we already had a packed programme for Easter, including a traditional joint sunrise service on the Friday morning which would have clashed with her suggestion.

Unfortunately, in a multicultural church, the willingness to make compromises – and even give up personal preferences which are based on aspects of our cultural identity – for the sake of the community always has to be stronger than the desire to have aspects of our own cultural identity valued and reaffirmed. This is only possible through humility and by focusing our attention on Jesus Christ, the one who teaches that it is better to give than to receive!

Conclusion: Looking towards the future

As I served in Thamesmead, I became totally convinced that God had been shaping me so that I could be better prepared to serve multicultural intergenerational churches. I also realised that my time serving as an assistant pastor at Thamesmead was part of the training for that specific calling, but that time was coming to an end. As I completed my fourth year serving at Thamesmead and also turned 31, it became clear to me that it was time to move on and assume the lead position in a church. Even more specifically, I felt that God was calling me to serve Him in Germany.

I started to pray and explore some possibilities and, sooner than I thought, a church in Germany became very interested in having me work with them. The church was very close to calling me, but in my final interview a problem surfaced. The leaders of the church wanted to continue to be very strict in the way they received and included members from other Christian denominations. I took the approach of being much more flexible. Things did not work out and therefore I returned to London, disappointed and frustrated. I asked God, 'Why did it go wrong?'

Then I felt that God responded, 'You do not need to push doors; I am the one who opens doors and closes doors.' From that moment on, I stopped contacting churches in Germany, believing that if God wanted me there, he would open the right door at the right time.

Time passed, and a few months later someone that I did not know saw a CV that I had sent to a Baptist organisation months before. Believing God was guiding them, this person wrote to me encouraging me to apply for the pastoral position at Bethel International Baptist Church in Frankfurt, Germany. It was God opening the door! This was a very interesting church – a multicultural, intergenerational, English-speaking church at the financial heart of Germany, belonging to the International Baptist Convention. More than 20 different nations are represented in the congregation, which is made up of people from varied socio-economic groups, including refugees and diplomats.

I applied for the post and went through a long process of questionnaires, interviews, preaching and conversations. Some time later I was told that, out of almost 30 candidates, I was to be the next pastor of the church. I was very surprised and at one point I asked them, 'Why me?' They said, 'All the candidates were very similar in their abilities and all of them are surely excellent pastors. You stood out because 1) you had experience working in a multicultural church and are committed to that vision; 2) you are in a mixed marriage; and 3) you said you would come to establish your family here and, hopefully, spend a considerable number of years serving with us. So, rationally, we could give you all these reasons to explain why you were chosen. However, the real reason is a spiritual one: we have been praying together and God has shown to us very clearly that you are to be our minister.'

That answer was convincing, comforting and challenging all at the same time.

I concluded my ministry and left the church in Thamesmead in December 2012. It was very difficult to leave behind so many people who are dear to us, but it was also exciting to know that God has new challenges ahead for me.

As I would only start serving in Frankfurt from around August 2013, another multicultural church in south-east London – Woolwich Central Baptist Church – invited me to help them as an interim pastor from January to July. This has been an amazing experience and I have been able to apply several lessons from my previous pastorate. I have been able to help them develop pastoral duties and support them in finding a suitable permanent pastor.

I am really looking forward to the future. I pray that God will bless me and give me more of His grace and more of His wisdom as I lead this wonderful multicultural, intergenerational church in Frankfurt. I pray too for His guidance, as I feel He is also calling me to step out and share more about multicultural ministry in the near future. I sense that God might also be calling me to get involved in the leadership council of the International Baptist Convention, to write more about the dynamics of multicultural churches, to take part in other conferences, to share my experiences and to give support and advice to other churches. We will have to wait and see what God's plans are.

Reflections

Rodrigo's story is significant in several ways. His family history and his grandfather's journey to faith remind us of the efforts and labour of European missionaries in Brazil and other parts of the world. His grandfather was led to Christ and baptised by an English Baptist missionary, and Rodrigo has now been here in England ministering in a Baptist church. This truly reflects the drama of reverse missions.

Another significance is that his story challenges the stereotype that South American immigrants in Britain are economic migrants. He had a good job in Brazil before coming to the UK to engage in mission. Also, he was already involved in ministry and mission in Brazil and Mozambique before coming to the UK, and this prepared him for ministry in Britain. This is important in demonstrating that God was already using him before he came to the UK. His missionary call to Wales is of importance as well, as he was invited to come by a Welsh indigene.

Another issue to take note of in Rodrigo's story is the fact that when he was moving from Wales to London and his ministerial credentials were sent out to Baptist churches in London, several different churches responded. This demonstrates that some British churches recognise the need for foreign missionaries or ministers to help the churches in the UK in regard to mission.

Rodrigo's time at Thamesmead really stretched his ministry as he came to grapple with issues of leadership and conflict resolution in a multicultural context. His ministry at Thamesmead demonstrates that not all Brazilian pastors are ministering to Brazilian congregations in the UK, as the church at Thamesmead is truly a multicultural church. In addition, his ministry among the youth and the church in general has been very productive as a result of his boldness and willingness to experiment with new ideas and new ways of doing things. Finally, God is now leading Rodrigo to lead an English-speaking multicultural church in Germany, opening his ministry even further and into Europe!

Chapter Three
My journey in the kingdom:
a Brazilian missionary in Northern Ireland
José Carlos Lara

It was a typical Brazilian autumn day in our school: dark and raining outside, students tired from working all day and facing a lot of study that night. Everything was calm, but someone was missing: our friend Dilcéia. She was a joyful girl and kept everyone's spirits high wherever she was. She was part of our gang and she had been missing from classes for a week.

Three of us decided to pay a visit to Dilcéia and see what was going on. So that evening we went to her house; I had no idea how much my life would change after that seemingly insignificant visit. At a time when there was no internet, PCs or mobiles (even the telephone was not very common in the average Brazilian household), the only way to talk to people was by going and talking to them personally, and that was what we intended to do.

After a good 40-minute walk we finally arrived at Dilcéia's house. Immediately we realised that she was sick and not able to come back to school yet, so we began to talk about more trivial things such as music and TV shows. Her mom fixed some coffee for us (Brazilians love coffee). Suddenly somebody knocked at the door and another bunch of friends came to visit her as well. We did not know these guys. They were from Dilcéia's church and somehow we were impacted by that group of young people who transmitted so much joy and peace. After half an hour with them I realised that they had something different, something that I did not have.

The whole group was so spontaneous that I barely noticed when one of the girls took out a guitar and started singing. Naturally the others joined in the song, and after a few minutes they were all singing along. They were lively, contemporary Christian songs; I had never heard this type of music before. Growing up in a traditional Catholic family, the only idea of religious music I had was of old-fashioned hymns that did not excite me at all. The church I used to attend was very solemn and quiet; 'the house of God' had to be silent. I don't know why, but the church building was poorly illuminated. For me, religious people laughing and enjoying themselves was inconceivable. And here we were in front of a youth group who were overflowing with joy and singing contemporary Christian songs.

At the end of the evening, one of the guys said they would like to pray for my sick friend, and she agreed. We all closed our eyes and bowed our heads respectfully waiting for the prayer. I secretly was expecting something like *Hail Mary* or some other repetition that I had learned, but the guy started to pray like someone who was talking to God like a friend, or a beloved father. It was so amazingly weird for me. In the beginning I was feeling awkward among all those young Christians praying out loud, one after the other, as if they were really enjoying themselves. But by the end I thought it was their way of showing some care to my friend, and I liked that.

As I went home with my two other friends, we talked about what had happened, and I realised that one of them was also impacted by what he saw. The other one was already a Christian and he had simply enjoyed the fellowship of the others. This was the beginning of a whole new life that was opening in front of me.

As a typical teenager, I did not mention anything to my parents, and life went on as normal. We would visit our friend more or less twice a week, and one day her friends invited me to visit their church for a Saturday night youth service. Bear in mind that we were living in the 1980s and were still under huge influence from John Travolta's movies and the whole disco movement, which meant that Saturday night was the peak of my week – the time to meet girls and hang out with friends. But that invitation struck me right in my heart; deep inside I knew that those boys and girls from the church were far happier than I was, and I wanted to be like them. I wanted to have the same joy and purpose in life. Before that I had tried to find a reason for life in Communism, through reading lots of books and dreaming about a just and beautiful utopia. I had also flirted with Eastern religions and meditation, and I felt that my own religion was just a bunch of rituals and empty words that did not make any sense to me. I had never made use of any illicit drugs, and the closest I came to a strange experience was a mix of tablets and alcohol that made me see some strange characters for few minutes and left me with a massive hangover afterwards.

As Saturday approached, I had to make a decision, and in the end I was determined to go to that church full of young people. It would be my first visit to an evangelical church, and it was very strange to me. I was expecting a traditional church building with poor illumination and terrible acoustic reverberation. But, on the contrary, the church was in a house that used to belong to a carpenter. The service was led by the youth and there was no pastor.

It was a strange experience for me to be in a church of a different denomination. The people there were very loving and happy. The picture of a church I had had in my mind was quiet prayer, very old hymns accompanied by an equally old organ and a priest saying complicated words that had nothing to do with my reality. But in that evangelical church, everything was the opposite of that concept. The building was light and simple, with clean walls and no icons or anything like that. The guys from the band (yes, they had a band!) played electric guitar, modern keyboard, and drums… unbelievable… drums in the church – it was surreal for me! This was June 1980.

The message was straightforward and brutally honest, with no complicated words, and directed to everyday people. God loves me, I am a sinner and I need to repent and accept Jesus as my saviour. That was so different for me. In contrast with my previous church it was like going to a theme park: the people there were happy instead of being silent and circumspect.

I continued to go to that church for a few weeks and my mum became suspicious about that; she said that it was not good to visit a church from a different religion. When she learned that I was going to a 'protestant' church she was very upset, and her first reaction was to talk to the priest of her church. The priest advised her that I was only following a fashion, influenced by peer group behaviour; it was only a teenage phase and soon I would return to my senses. Some friends and family members said that 'sects' were brainwashing young people in those days. My mum became angry…

I attended the services of that church for a few more weeks, and finally the time came when I accepted that I was a sinner and needed a saviour. It was a very cold Sunday night and I remember that there was a guest speaker that night. His name was Rene Feitosa and he had been the pastor and founder of a great church in Belo Horizonte (almost 600km away from Sao Paulo where I was living at that time). Peniel Church was well known for their work among drug addicts, prostitutes, homosexuals and the homeless in the so-called Great Belo Horizonte. On that night he preached about Jesus as a cornerstone, and I realised that I needed to put my trust in Jesus Christ, not only as my saviour but also as my cornerstone, the foundation of my life, my King and my Lord.

When Pastor Rene asked if anyone wanted to surrender his life to the Lord, I really wanted to do that, but somehow a struggle was going on in my mind. People started to pray for me and ask for deliverance, and then I noticed that I was at the front of the church with my hand raised, crying like a baby. But they were good tears. At the same time, I was conscious of my sin and had a deep sense of repentance. I also had an inexplicable feeling of joy running all over my body. It was like someone taking a yoke off my shoulders. An explosion of tears and joy came upon me... I knew that something had happened inside me, something that would change my life forever.

Soon I was involved with the youth ministry of that church. One day, during a congress in a town far away from Sao Paulo I heard for the first time about world missions. The testimony and the preaching of that world mission congress ignited a passion that has continued to push me for the last 30 years.

Two years later I met Mari, the girl who would become my wife. Even during our first conversations I made clear to her that I had a strong sense of a call from God to work in the mission field. Being a missionary from the third world meant I would probably never have a good salary or be able to give her material comfort or riches. She told me that she also felt that she had a missionary call and she would follow me wherever the Lord would take us. After all this time she is still my wife, my girlfriend and my biggest supporter as we worked together as partners in ministry. We have three wonderful daughters who fill the house with joy! They have also learnt to share in the pains and struggles that sometimes follow the families of missionaries. My family is my biggest blessing and source of encouragement.

Once we got engaged we planned to begin our missionary careers. In our naive minds, typical of a 20-year-old couple, we had planned to go as a missionary couple on Operation Mobilisation's Doulos Ship. This ship is a multi-Christian ministry ship that does a fantastic job in terms of evangelism, social work, training for pastors and leaders and support for local churches. They divide their team of volunteer missionaries into different styles of ministry, and they have an amazing impact wherever they go. We wanted to serve the Lord with all our youthful passion and strength, but without any of the planning or training that cross-cultural mission work demands.

We served as volunteers while the ship was in Santos, Brazil. The atmosphere of a ship with 300 people from more than 50 different countries on board was simply fantastic; I couldn't resist its charming blend of cultures. If I had any doubt about my missionary call it was dissipated over those two weeks.

Things began to turn a bit sour when we went to talk to the director of personnel who explained that the ship's rules stated that engaged couples were not allowed to become missionaries for a two-year period. Either we had to separate and only one of us would be accepted, or we had to get married first and then present for selection again.

We decided to get married, as this was already in our plans, with the hope that the ship would recruit us the following year. With this plan in mind we did not buy much furniture or even consider long-term jobs. We decided to live a very spartan lifestyle for our first few months of marriage because we were absolutely sure that we would soon be serving the Lord as missionaries on board the Doulos ship. My mother-in-law had a small business at that time and she employed me for the period until we would go onto the ship.

The recruitment and selection conference arrived, and we were there trying to accomplish our missionary dream. The moment of truth had finally come, and we were very excited.

However, the situation had changed. Just a few months after we married, my wife became pregnant. Decisions now had to be made taking into consideration three people instead of two.

The interview with the director of personnel took place at a Christian conference and retreat centre in Rio Bonito, Rio de Janeiro State. The heat was unbearable and I remember that we were both sweating a lot. Although the interviewer was very polite, he was also very direct, and affirmed that the ship could not take a pregnant woman; only emergency medical treatment was carried out on board. Therefore they could not accept us, for the second time. This was a second major disappointment in just over a year.

The following year they had another recruitment conference in Brazil, but as my wife was expecting our second daughter at this time, we decided not to go and to accept the fact that it was not God's will for us to work as missionaries on that ship. Soon after, we decided to move to another church. That two-year period had been significantly hurtful for us and it was very clear that our small and beloved home church had no structure to send out missionaries. We tried to talk to the president of the missionary association of our denomination. He made it very clear that their priority was national missions and that they had no financial resources to spare for international mission.

My wife had grown up in a bigger church where the pastor was very passionate about world mission and was one of the leaders of the new missionary movement that had started in Brazil in around 1984. That church welcomed us, and the first thing we did was to talk to the pastor about our missionary calling and our passion for the Lord Jesus Christ and His work. He congratulated us as he opened a drawer in his desk and gave us a brochure that said:

> We will be delighted to send you as a missionary couple from this church. But [there is always a 'but'!], we have a department of missions in our church and they have prepared a missionary training programme that is about to start.

Without thinking or reading the brochure, I said, 'I'm in! When do we start?' And we started training on that very day.

The missionary training programme took ten years to complete; this included theology, missiology and theoretical teaching as well as practical training, and all sorts of other experiences that you can imagine. In our local church we worked with the discipleship programme, children in the Sunday School classes and the youth band. After that, I took the exam of the council of that denomination, and after five exhaustive hours of questioning I was approved by a unanimous vote of the pastors present. In the next few weeks I was ordained a minister.

After planting a church in a town in Sao Paulo State, we were finally commissioned and sent by our home church to Britain, about 12 years after we were rejected by the Doulos ship. According to the tradition of our local church, the whole family – my wife, our three daughters and myself – were called to the front of the church to receive a blessing and the commitment of that church to our family and ministry. Perhaps the most important aspect of it all was that the church was accepting the responsibility of taking care of our family – spiritually, emotionally and financially.

North Wales and England

Finally the great day had arrived. After an 11-hour flight, our family arrived at Heathrow Airport along with two other Brazilian missionaries heading for the same Missionary Language School in north Wales (by coincidence, or 'God-incidence', the school was part of the same mission as the Doulos ship).

We were tired and at the same time overexcited about the new life that lay ahead of us. Everything was new: the colours and sounds around us, people speaking different languages, and faces of people from literally all over the world. Heathrow Airport can be a very interesting and exciting place, especially if you are a first-time visitor.

We were taken to the Mission's house to have a night's rest, then from Victoria Station we took a bus to Rhyl, north Wales, where we joined all the other students from across the world. We spent about a year in that school and, after some interesting experiences with other students and teachers, we all survived the so-called cross-cultural shock. I realise now that the time we spent in that school was extremely important to build the foundation of our future ministry in the United Kingdom.

After the first year in Wales we were moved to Hastings in East Sussex, where I was put to work with an organisation that used to give training in Christian discipleship. It was a difficult time for me personally. I had to spend most of my time in an office despite the fact that I was trained to be – and had expected to be – a church planter. I also had many disagreements with the leadership. On reflection, I think that the whole situation was mismanaged; we were all immature and we could have found a better way of solving those issues. But the decision at that time was that we should return to Brazil. So we did.

We spent the following five years trying to rebuild our lives, our reputation, our relationship with our church and also our ministry. The five years we spent in Brazil was also a time for us as a family for healing our wounds and maturing as God's people.

After the restoration process, the time came to be sent again to the mission field. The opportunity to come back to Britain came in 2003 when I went to a Restoration Retreat for missionaries that was held at my former school of missions (Evangelical Missionary Centre in Viçosa-MG). There I met a lady called Claire Siddaway, the Director of Latin Partners, the branch of Latin Link that is responsible for missionaries who come from Latin America to work in Europe. She told me that there were opportunities for Brazilian missionaries in the UK, and a few weeks later she informed me of an opportunity for ministry in Northern Ireland.

I was very curious about this opportunity; the only thing I knew about Northern Ireland was what I heard on the news channels in Brazil that talked about bombings, killings, terrorist attacks and those sorts of things. But God was at work in our hearts, and after a period of prayer we decided to accept it as God's direction for our life and ministry.

A lot of things had changed in our church since we had first been sent. The senior pastor had been dismissed and the church was being administered by a council of pastors and leaders of the different ministries of the church. The financial situation was also very difficult, and the leaders of the council said they could only pray for us and bless our sending, giving us support in prayer but unfortunately not financially. At that stage we had a clear sense of calling and therefore we would not let anything impede our accomplishing it. We decided to accept it and believe that somehow God would provide for us.

We did not have the money to buy the air tickets so we left our jobs, sold some of our furniture and gave away the rest. But all the money put together was not enough to pay for five tickets from Sao Paulo to Belfast. We prayed about this and shared the need with friends and churches that we knew. Our flight was scheduled to leave on Sunday 1st February 2004, and the manager of the travel agency phoned me the week before to say that if we did not deposit the money before 4.30pm on Friday the tickets would be void. We had already said goodbye to family and friends, my wife and I had left our jobs, our daughters had left their schools and the church had blessed us for our missionary journey.

The Friday arrived and we were still lacking a substantial part of the money. I was really concerned, and a million questions were going through my mind: what if we do not get the money? How can I face my family, my church, and my colleagues whom I told I was going to be a missionary in Ireland? Where could we live without a house, a job, or even the necessary food to eat?

I had hoped that some people would deposit money in our bank account, but when I went to the bank at about 4pm the ATM screen showed the opposite; the miracle had not happened. I was lacking about US $1,000 to complete the payment for the tickets. I would love to say that my faith was strong and I knew that the Lord would provide for us, but I was not feeling that way; I was very disappointed and frustrated. At that moment I thought that everything was lost.

Fifteen minutes later I checked the balance again, and some small deposits had started to come into the account from different branches and different people! The deposits continued to add up until 4.25pm when the whole amount for the tickets had finally arrived. I transferred the money to the travel agency at 4.30pm sharp. Thank God for His provision and care that does not depend on our feelings or emotions. Glory be to Him only!

With the daily needs of my family at the back of my mind, I understood that with a student visa I could work part-time, and my wife and daughters could eventually work to provide for the house. At that stage, the most important thing was the conviction of the direction of God for our family, and that He was calling us to Northern Ireland.

A lot of people came to the airport for the final farewell, and it was a sight that will be in my mind for many years. Brothers and sisters from our church came, along with family members and friends. Some people were carrying banners, some were singing, and my mother and other relatives were crying. Some people came to me, and while they hugged me they put some money in my pocket. When we were finally on board I counted the money in my pocket. It was £240, and thinking in terms of Brazilian currency, I thought this money would be enough to live on for a few weeks. I soon realised that the exchange rate of 2004 could be a nasty foe of a Brazilian missionary in the UK!

Northern Ireland (2004)

The date was 2nd February 2004. It was a typical winter twilight, a cold and dark Monday evening, when we arrived at Belfast City Airport. By mistake I misinformed the person who would meet our family at the airport and told him we would arrive at the International Airport, about 30 miles away! I quickly rearranged this and we were very happy to see Richard and Keith arrive with two large cars to welcome us and take us to our new home. Keith would become my partner in ministry for the next five years, and it was he who led us on our first steps in this new country.

We arrived at the flat that had been reserved for us late that night, and the landlord's wife had kindly prepared a meal for us.

We were all exhausted but happy. The landlord was a mature Christian called Ivan who ran a convenience shop in a neighbourhood about three miles from the town centre. It was clear that many Christians knew we were there and they soon helped us to settle in. Almost every evening a Christian would visit us and bring food, and sometimes in the mornings we found little envelopes containing money that would help us in difficult times. We had arrived with £240, and after two months we still had £240! Praise the Lord!

After a while we became involved with the local Baptist church and also visited some Presbyterian churches nearby. Living in that place was good for us, but it was expensive as we had to get the bus to the churches and the town centre. We were quite happy there until we saw stickers in public places with racist messages, including the classic 'niggers out'. It took me a few minutes to realise that the only dark-skinned people living in the whole neighbourhood were my wife and one of my daughters, although given the average Northern Irish skin colour, my whole family would be considered coloured people. This was quite new for me because in Brazil people mix with and get married to literally every race and colour. Our country is like a huge melting pot with people coming from all over the world. When I was a child, I was blonde with blue eyes and I used to be called *alemão* (meaning German) by other boys, so now being a target of racism seemed absurd to me. We decided to move to another place.

A brother from the Baptist church offered us a house to rent in the town centre at a very low cost. This gentleman had a funeral home and the house was attached to it, with interconnecting doors. After a few weeks we moved into that house, which was very good for us.

I attended one of our (Latin Link) mission conferences in Bangor and we had a really good time of sharing, prayer and mutual encouragement. During the lunch I sat beside a kind gentleman and we began to talk. He was one of the prayer supporters of Latin Link and we had been chatting for about half an hour when he asked me, 'Do you have a car?' and I replied that we did not. He then asked me a second question: 'Would you like to have one?'

I said, 'Sure.' He then explained that his daughter had an extra car and would like to donate it to a missionary. I just thought: 'Praise the Lord!'

The car arrived on a Friday, and after we had sorted all the papers and insurance, I finally had a car. I was happy about the way it could enlarge the reach of our ministry and make things easier at home as well. Taking the children to school and doing shopping would be much simpler now.

Two days after receiving the car we had to take my daughter to an out-of-hours doctor in a town nearby. My daughter had contracted a disease that left her body totally paralysed from the neck down. After all these years, I still do not know exactly what she had. The doctor just said that it *could be* some type of virus. Those days were really difficult for us: we had to carry her to the bathroom and my wife had to feed and wash her. For a girl who was 17 years old, you may guess that this was a very difficult time. Fortunately it only went on for a week, but that week was probably the most difficult since we had arrived in the UK, and it was just the beginning.

During that same week, a Christian group had organised a joint service between Catholics and Protestants at Dungannon Park, and they invited me to take part. There would be no preaching, only songs of praise and Bible readings, and I would read the final prayer. I thought that this was a good idea, especially in the context of Northern Ireland where the religious conflict had caused so much pain and hatred. I accepted the invitation and made it clear that although I would not define myself as ecumenical, I believe in the unity of the church and do not support any sectarian activities.

The following day, an elder from one of the churches that supported us called me to express his concerns about me attending that event. After a brief conversation I explained that I did not think there was anything in the Bible that forbade me to go to a service like that, and that we as Christians should support actions like that instead of supporting division among people. He finished the conversation by saying that the Protestants would not be happy about it. On the next two evenings, some other folk from both churches phoned me advising me not to go to the event. One of them was very emphatic and said, 'We do not share the pulpit with a priest.' I tried to clarify that the priest would not be there, but that even if he was I would not be 'contaminated' by his Catholicism.

The service in the park was beautiful, with a good crowd enjoying themselves singing praises to the Lord and listening to the Bible readings. At the end I read the final prayer, and I had a really good time there. After the service we had some refreshments and I met some new people. It was great! After I arrived home I spent some time talking with my wife, and then we went to bed.

It was just after 5am when somebody knocked on our door. I jumped from my bed trying to figure out what was going on. When I opened the door it was raining and dark, and a fireman was standing in front of me.

'Do you have a grey Ford Escort parked at the rear?'

'Yes... Why?'

'Please get dressed and follow me.'

I was in my pyjamas and was trying to guess what had happened.

When we went to the car park at the rear of the house I had a big shock. Our newly donated car had been destroyed by fire and was still exhaling some smoke. I walked around the car searching for something that could be saved from the fire, and a few metres from the car I found my Bible. Whoever did this had taken the Bible out of the car and burnt the car, leaving a clear message for me.

That night we were awakened by the noise of stones being thrown at our windows, and the same thing happened the following night. We phoned the police and they sent a car that stayed throughout the night, and the noise stopped.

We tried to figure out who had done this to us and why, and there were several possibilities. First, that the radical Protestant groups did it because they were not happy with my taking part in an ecumenical event. Second, that this was a racist attack: we were foreigners and my wife and daughter have dark skin. Third, that it was a random attack: the car was in the wrong place at the wrong time.

After the attacks we started to make contact with other Portuguese speakers in the town. We discovered that we could find many of them in the local library because most had no computers at home and they could access the internet for free there.

Another place where we could find immigrants was at an English class for foreign people. At that class we met a lady who began to attend our meetings. There was a Gospel Hall in Dungannon and the people there had realised that the town was rapidly changing and a lot of Portuguese speakers were living nearby and working in the local meat factories. They had the clever idea of putting up a sign in Portuguese inviting people to their services. We went to visit that church and I presented myself as a minister and missionary whose aim was to reach out to the Portuguese and Brazilian communities in that town. They were very polite but said that we could not work together because they believed that only people who belonged to their church were saved (after the service during the refreshments a lady asked me if I was saved).

The best thing that happened on that day was meeting Junior and Kelly. They were a very nice young Brazilian couple, also visiting that church for the first time, and we invited them to our home for a cup of coffee. They came, and after some time chatting we invited them to study the Bible with us. They happily accepted and asked if they could bring some friends, and soon we had started a Bible study group in the lounge of the house.

This was our first year and it was hard, but we learnt a lot about the Northern Irish culture and the Christian evangelical subculture in Northern Ireland.

By the second year, our Bible study group was too big for our lounge, so we decided to move to the premises of the Drop-in Centre of Dungannon Youth for Christ. It was a blessing for us that they accepted us because we could use the room as well as the table tennis, the video games and the snooker table. This made it far easier to invite young people to come for our meetings. The venue also had a small kitchen where we would prepare tea, coffee and sandwiches for after the study.

In that place, many people were saved, comforted, encouraged and challenged. It was in that year that we realised that one of the needs of the Portuguese speakers was to learn the English language. For five years in Brazil my wife and I had both worked as English teachers, and that experience could now be applied in this new context. So we began to teach English to foreigners for free.

We received our first helper in that second year; his name was Pedro Paulo and he was a blessing to us. The plan was for him to work in the meat factory of the town where most of the migrant workers were, and there he would be a witness for Christ in the work environment. He would be able to make contacts and evangelise the non-Christians, as well as support himself by working there. It worked very well, and the time he spent in Dungannon blessed the whole immigrant community.

A few months later we received a team of six young people who would do basically the same thing that Pedro Paulo had done. At this stage the Bible study group was big enough to start a service in the Portuguese language. We talked with leaders of one of the churches that supported the project among the immigrants, and they agreed to lend us their church hall for us to hold our services in Portuguese. So we had English lessons and Bible study on Saturdays and the service on Sundays. There were people from Brazil, Portugal, Angola, Mozambique, Cape Verde and East Timor.

This new team of young men and women helped us in the services and the Bible studies and also worked in factories in the same way that Pedro Paulo did.

At the end of the year, we wanted to put on a Christmas play. We planned to use a play that my wife and I had written when we worked in the children's ministry in our home church back in Brazil. We had to remember the plot, rewrite the script and select the cast and those who would work behind the scenes. The rhythm of the rehearsals was becoming more and more intense as the day of the presentation approached. The youth support team that came from our church were all engaged, and we saw that multi-talented youth group in action.

We had advertised the play extensively in both churches (Baptist and Presbyterian) and among the immigrants as well. The play was a mix of musical, humour and drama, and was the story of two immigrants who came to Northern Ireland, one of whom was arrested and then repented and was saved in prison. The message was contextualised and had a link with the audience.

On the evening the play was performed, we had a good crowd of foreigners and some members of the churches (perhaps more out of curiosity than to show support), and the hall of the Baptist church was packed, so we all felt that our efforts had paid off. The whole team knew that the message had reached the heart of the immigrants, and we were very happy with that indescribable feeling of mission accomplished. It had such an impact that Keith invited us to present the same play at the Presbyterian Church. Although it was logistically impossible at that time, the following year we presented a different Christmas drama at the Presbyterian hall.

At this stage, the reputation of the ministry was growing, and I was invited to do interviews with a radio programme and the local newspaper. Churches would often call Keith or me to speak about the project and we challenged them to take part. After a while, we offered English lessons for immigrants in Cookstown and Magherafelt as well as Dungannon.

When we opened the doors of the church and invited the 'non-churchgoers', they came, and soon after we began to provide English lessons for the foreign mothers. Keith thought that we could use the same venue, resources and volunteers of the local church to provide a crèche for the children of those learning English. However, problems were inevitable, and after a few weeks some volunteers threatened to boycott the crèche if we kept bringing the 'black children' to 'their' crèche. Keith wisely managed the situation, changing the day of our classes to a different day of the week. In this way we could keep the venue, but we had to find some helpers to look after the children. The following week we both brought our daughters to be the helpers, and this solved the problem.

Every week we provided some refreshments for the children and mothers – simple things such as tea and coffee for the adults and squash with biscuits for the children. But a few days after the problem with the church volunteers, we were surprised to find that the beakers were locked in a cupboard in the church kitchen. Initially we thought that there had been a misunderstanding and that they had been locked away by mistake, but when Keith went to talk to the person in charge, she replied that they did not want to share the beakers with the black children, fearing contamination.

That was one of the worst days of our ministry there. How could a person who calls herself a Christian be so racist? But we had to keep going.

Attendance at the English classes, Bible study and services was increasing. We started to teach some of the deeper aspects of Christian doctrine about commitment and discipleship, and the pathway for baptism was launched for the new converts.

At this time it became clear that the local church's perception of our work was different from our own. I thought of our ministry as a 'church planting ministry', and therefore I saw us as an independent immigrant church that had the local church's support and worked alongside them. However, from the local church's point of view, we were part of their church and therefore should submit to their decisions. When I realised this I tried to emphasise the need for keeping the language and culture of the immigrants, as that would be crucial to maintaining their identity. With these two different views of the same ministry, and dealing with cultural and religious differences, the clashes were inevitable.

For instance, it is quite common to find migrant workers who have no visa or work permit. I believe that when a person in such a situation is willing to be baptised, he/she like any other sinner should be welcomed, supported, loved, baptised and accepted into the church. But the elders of our partner church forbade us to baptise them because they were illegal immigrants. However, another church came to rescue us in that situation and we had the baptisms there. In total we baptised 15 people during the first three years of our ministry in Dungannon.

In my mind was always this concept of the conversion circle:

1) A person recognises his state of sin and soul in need and repents.

2) A person converts in a decision to become a disciple of Christ.

3) A person is accepted, loved and supported by the church. He or she is baptised if they express the desire to do so.

4) The sanctification (or in other words the pathway of a holy life) will be a process of leaving the past, bad habits and sins that

entangle his/her Christian life. This is a journey that will take a lifetime, therefore we should not expect someone to beat all the sins in his/her life at once or to behave in certain manner in order to be accepted into the church through baptism. Discipleship should be developed in different spheres of church life, such as personal discipleship (one-to-one), small groups and congregational meetings.

We had a profound debate with the local leaders who thought that 'illegal immigrants' should not be baptised. The debate went along two different strands:

a) *The Bible says that we have to obey the law of the land, therefore if one does not have the right type of visa he is breaking the law, and as a consequence he is sinning.* However, I do not see in the Bible that to work without a visa or a work permit is worse than driving on the motorway above the speed limit, or not paying your taxes, or looking lustfully at a woman. These are all sins, and if we were to follow this rule we would not see a single Christian being baptised. Simple as that. These sins or bad behaviour are personal struggles that everyone has to fight, and with the help of God we will progress in our Christian journey.

b) *Yes we have to obey the law of the land, but what if the law is against the very character of God?* It is very helpful for British Christians to understand this by reflecting on the situation in which Christians were living in Nazi Germany during the Second World War when they had to disobey the laws of the Nazi regime because some were clearly racist, unfair and, of course, against the law of God. When we examine immigration laws today in most Western countries, the primary objective is to protect the national borders, and this is often to the detriment of the foreigner who is seen as a second-class person. The national citizen is assumed to be better than the foreign national, who is often viewed with suspicion. My big question is, 'Does the immigration law in the UK reflect the character of God or His values?' Or is it just accepted as common sense, and in fact reflects the values of a society that is increasingly secular and ungodly and stigmatises immigrants? I am aware that this is controversial, but it is important to reflect on the issues of immigration and not just accept the dominant discourse.

These are just some of the arguments we had with the evangelical leadership of that town. The fact is that after this, my relationships with the local evangelical churches were becoming increasingly cold and distant. The invitations I used to have to speak in other churches, Christian camps and Christian meetings reduced. Somehow people saw me as a pastor who accepted the illegal immigrants in his church, and as a consequence I guess people saw me as the 'illegal pastor'.

In a church working with immigrants, the attendance is very irregular due to the nature of the migrant worker lifestyle. It is a bit like an airport: people come and go all the time, but only a few are there to stay. When we arrived in 2004, the average time of an immigrant in Northern Ireland was two years. During these two years the mentality was 'work as much as you can, earn as much as you can and save as much as you can'. It was especially difficult if we were planning to train leadership for the future. But in the end we had to accept the fact that our 'wee church' had its own characteristics.

Everything was going well, notwithstanding the normal struggles already mentioned, until the recession in 2008. Suddenly our small church that had an attendance of around 60 people every Sunday service started to lose people. Almost every month we lost some people, as entire families decided to move back to their countries or go somewhere else because they simply lost their jobs and could not afford to pay the rent. In 2009 there was only one couple left, and we realised that our time in Dungannon had come to an end.

Those years of ministry in Dungannon were full of blessings, and full of struggles as well, and it is strange to see how attractive the struggles of Christian life and ministry are in retrospect. There were some disappointments, but also a joy that is indescribable. A joy when you see other churches in the country doing the same thing you started as a pioneer. A joy of seeing people who have had their lives transformed by the power of God, and somehow you feel you are a part of it. All the glory and praise be to God!

One of our daughters had planned her wedding for September 2009, and we waited until after her wedding before we moved to Belfast. We as a family still felt the direction of God to remain in the country, hence we stayed in the UK and specifically in Northern Ireland, but I was eager for new challenges. In Belfast we visited many churches until we found a charismatic, multi-ethnic and non-sectarian church in east Belfast. What caught my eye was that in that church we could see people from many different nationalities – different skin colours, different races and different cultural backgrounds. It all added to the contemporary music and a contextualised message of the gospel. They had all that I was looking for.

The church in general welcomed us, and the senior pastor gave me freedom to work among the foreigners. It was a bit difficult in the beginning because in Dungannon I had been the missionary and the pastor of a church that I had founded, and now the circumstances had changed and we had become members of a well-established church in east Belfast. As such, I was just another person, a member like anyone else.

Today, we run a Bible study group in Portuguese. We also have a monthly meeting called International Lunch where we welcome, offer support to and reach out to the foreign community in Belfast. During the summer months of 2012 we ran a football tournament with teams made up of immigrants from Brazil, Angola, Poland, Slovakia and a team from our church. Occasionally my wife and I do some chaplaincy work in prisons and hospitals, and I am also dedicating a large part of my time to writing.

We pray that somehow my story can contribute to a better understanding of the foreign community living in the UK. It is so diverse and so colourful that it presents one of the biggest challenges to the twenty-first-century church in Britain. How can a local church, living in postmodern European society, understand, welcome, support and reach out to the foreigners living on the doorsteps of the church?

I believe we are living a re-enactment of Acts 2 in Europe today:

> Now there were staying in Jerusalem God-fearing Jews from every nation under heaven. (Acts 2:5)

In the same way, it seems that God is bringing people from all over the world to the countries of the North Atlantic, especially the big cities. Now is the time for the church to respond like Peter did:

> Then Peter stood up with the Eleven, raised his voice and addressed the crowd. (Acts 2:14)

The time has come to stand up, united, to raise our voice and address the crowd. I believe we still have a relevant message for the world, and it has to be preached in the most diverse ways for all the nations around us and beyond.

The consequence of it will be like in the book of Acts:

> When the people heard this, they were cut to the heart and said to Peter and the other apostles, 'Brothers, what shall we do?' Peter replied, 'Repent and be baptised, every one of you, in the name of Jesus Christ for the forgiveness of your sins. And you will receive the gift of the Holy Spirit. The promise is for you and your children and for all who are far off – for all whom the Lord our God will call.' (Acts 2:37-39)

Reflections

José Carlos Lara's story is not just about an individual doing mission; rather it is the story of his whole family getting involved in mission. This started back in Brazil when he and his wife first heard God's call to be missionaries. José Carlos and Mari's story reveals that there are times when God calls the family and not just the individual. They met with lots of opposition in Brazil in fulfilling their missionary call, but this appears to have strengthened them and trained them for the tasks ahead.

It is important to note that José was ordained as a minister in Brazil before coming to the UK. He also planted and pastored a church before coming to the UK. What is interesting is that, despite the fact that they were on their first mission trip to the UK, their local church in Brazil supported them financially, spiritually and emotionally. This is quite significant as their sending church took responsibility and did not just leave it in the hands of people in Wales, or the family themselves.

Their call to Northern Ireland was through Latin Partners, which is a part of Latin Link. Latin Link's work is very important in regard to reverse mission as they have been sending and facilitating missionaries coming from South America to Britain for the last ten years.

Another consideration is that both of their calls to Britain were to places outside of London. This challenges the notion that ethnic minority pastors and missionaries are looking for easy and comfortable places such as London or other large multi-ethnic cities.

José Carlos's family have had a fruitful ministry among the ethnic minorities in Northern Ireland against the backdrop of the divide between Catholics and Protestants. It is interesting that God has used them to minister to Brazilians and other foreign workers in Northern Ireland, showing that reverse mission to Britain does not always mean working primarily with British-born people. However, their ministry has also sought to bridge the gap between Northern Irish indigenes and the ethnic minorities who are perceived as 'others'. They have also worked alongside and supported indigenous church leaders as well as challenging practices in the church which they believe to be wrong and unbiblical.

Their perseverance and faithfulness in ministry, despite setbacks and racist attacks, shows the commitment and self-sacrifice which is such an integral part of so many reverse mission stories. An interesting question raised by their ministry experience in Northern Ireland is whether Britain's immigration laws are based on common human rights, or whether they are founded on nationalism and lead to racial discrimination, and are therefore counter to God's character and values.

SECTION B

AFRICA

A missionary from Nigeria to Britain
Jonathan Oloyede

**Multicultural churches in Britain:
the journey to Crofton Park Baptist Church**
Israel Olofinjana

Multi-ethnic or multicultural churches in Bristol?
Tayo Arikawe

A call to the nations
Peter Oyugi

Chapter Four
A missionary from Nigeria to Britain
Jonathan Oloyede

'Allah u Akbar, Allah u Akbar!' As the lead worshipper projected these words, we all bowed and kissed the floor with our foreheads. I was among 200 other Muslim worshippers in the local central mosque in Lagos during the month of Ramadan. As I walked home that evening with my uncle, a very devout Muslim, I was a mixed bag of emotions and questions.

I had just gained admission into university to study medicine and was the toast of the whole family and community to which I belonged. A lot of attention was being showered on me because I had suddenly become the high-water mark and showcase of the entire Oloyede clan. There were no other doctors in the family, from my generation or the generations before me, so it was a great pride to the family that we now were going to have a doctor in the house. So as I walked home with my uncle that evening, preparing for the unknown, I was asking myself: 'What is God like? Who is He? Can I relate to Him? What's medical school going to be like? I wonder what the other campus students are going to be like.'

'Jonathan you must always be a good Muslim,' my uncle began, snapping me back into the here and now. 'When you get on campus, keep your head and show those wayward kids what a good Muslim is like.' I recoiled inwardly, not at his words but at the intensity and vehemence with which he said them. Al Hajji Kassim, as he was popularly known, was my mum's younger brother, and he had a religious fanaticism that always put me on edge.

Within six months of campus life, after many months of internal confusion and various intense religious discussions with Christians on campus, I gave my life to Jesus. My conversion was more of an encounter than a decision. Many of my friends at the university were Christians who constantly invited me to the student fellowships. I constantly refused, reasoning that a good Muslim wouldn't step into a church.

One fateful night, I decided to try it out. The moment I stepped into the prayer service I had a very strange encounter. For many years as a devout Muslim, I would talk to God on my mat and in my heart and ask Him to relate to me. I would rant at Him, 'If you are real, why don't you speak to me? Why can't I relate with you? If you are so big and mighty, how come we human beings can talk to each other but you cannot talk to us?' As I walked into the room that night, I felt a strange, familiar presence, both in my heart and around me. I cannot explain it, but I just knew I was home.

In a matter of seconds my heart was resounding with the revelation, 'God is here!' That night I gladly received Jesus into my heart and was baptised in the Holy Spirit and began speaking in tongues. When I went to bed, I had an amazing dream. In the dream the student hostel that my friends and I were staying in suddenly caught fire and we were running for our lives. It was like one of the scenes from the movie *Backdraft*. As we raced up the stairs to escape the flames, we all came out on the flat roof of the building. It was a 40ft drop to the floor, and the next building was too far away to jump to. As the fire's intensity increased behind us, I heard a voice say to me, 'Jump.'

I turned in the direction of the voice, and said, 'It's impossible to jump this distance. No human being can do it.'

The voice simply responded, 'I said jump.' So, like Neo in *The Matrix*, I ran and jumped towards the next building and landed safely, to my utter surprise. I then turned to look back and saw my friends, helpless and hopeless at the mercy of the flames.

The voice then said to me, 'Pray for your friends.' So I dropped to my knees on the roof and began praying for my friends. When my knees touched the floor, I awoke with a start and sat up in bed. It seemed as if I could still hear the voice from the dream talking to me in my heart: 'Jonathan, you have been saved from the flames, the fire, you can now do what you couldn't do before. Begin to pray and intercede for your friends.'

From the moment of my conversion, I found out that God was real, very real. One by one, my friends gave their lives to Christ. Many of the people I prayed for had dramatic healing experiences or encounters. I would wake up in the morning and instantly know, without any communication whatsoever, that my parents were planning to come and visit. And sure enough, they would show up. God by his Holy Spirit began to commune with my heart in very real and intimate ways.

The one big nagging question was how I would tell my parents that I had become a Christian. I knew it was going to be a big problem, and it was. 'You are no longer my son!' my father shouted at me. 'In fact, I want you out of this house immediately!' My dad wasn't taking the news of my conversion lightly. His whole demeanour and attitude was quite hostile, frightening and confusing. Despite the pleas from my mum, he refused to back down. I left home and moved into a Christian community adjacent to the medical campus.

It was many months before my dad changed his mind. I later learnt that many of his friends were taking jabs at him because their sons were into girls and drugs while his had become a monk. They'd jokingly say to him, 'Chief, we like your problem. Can we exchange sons?'

On 11th November 2005, my dad slipped peacefully into eternity in his sleep. In the last two years of his life, he along with my mum had become Christians and faithful worshippers in my then church, Glory House. He was the last to receive Christ in my family, but the first to see Him face to face. Truly the last shall be the first. God does have a sense of humour!

Looking back, I can see how God had been guiding and moulding my life. Everything that has happened to me up till now, He had already whispered in my ear. Truly He is amazing in the way He leads and guides. One of my favourite passages can be found in one of David's psalms, which reads:

> Take delight in the Lord, and he will give you the desires of your heart. Commit your way to the Lord; trust in him and he will do this. (Psalm 37:4-5)

Somehow God has continued to bless me and give me things that I haven't asked for. I discover that when I ask for more of God, He comes with lots of Christmas presents. He is the real Santa Claus. He has blessed me with an immensely satisfying marriage, lovely children and deep, meaningful relationships. He has given me good health, honour, joy and profound peace.

My advice to all leaders is that they spend time in Psalm 23:2: 'He makes me lie down in green pastures, he leads me beside quiet waters.' The more time you can spend in His presence, the more of His presence will go, grow and glow in you. People will be attracted to you (for the right reasons), and something of eternal life will flow out from you into thirsty souls.

I want to know Jesus. I really want to meet Him before I die. It's a real passion that I have been given from God. I ask Him for His presence every day. I ask for His mercy and grace all the time. Somehow He is always ready to help me, to lift me up and strengthen me. I think one of the greatest secrets to succeeding as a leader is to stay really close to Jesus, all the time, in your heart, in your head and with your hands; in your motives, in your thinking and in your actions.

This desire and vision has taken on many forms, right from my days at medical school up till the present. I have been involved with Building Together for London, the Evangelical Alliance, Face Values, Oasis, Spring Harvest, Churches Together in England, Churches Together in Britain and Ireland, Newham Christian Fellowships, Faithworks, Newham Borough Deans, the African and Caribbean Evangelical Alliance, Charismatic Leaders Conferences, March for Jesus... The list goes on and on. I was also involved in building a network across London seeking to bring transformation through Soul in the City.

My vision is to see the church united for the Great Commission and transformation. Maybe I am a bit deluded or naive, but I believe it is possible for God's body of believers to work together in unity, no matter how hard it might be.

God's call to the UK

I arrived on an afternoon flight from Lagos, Nigeria, in the summer of 1991, returning to the place of my birth and childhood. My memory bank regularly replays the first glimpse of the green chequered English fields from my window seat in the Nigerian Airways flight. I remember thinking how idyllic the toy-sized houses looked, neatly arranged in rows; very different from the compact spaghetti slums of cosmopolitan Ibadan. Fresh from the tyrannical pressure of consistent rigorous study in medical school, I was well overdue for a holiday and change of scenery. I had decided to take a three-month holiday before embarking on my itinerant year at a renowned Baptist Training Hospital in the Islamic enclave of northern Nigeria. As a convert from Islam, my intention was to practise as a missionary doctor to Muslims in the region.

'Your sister would really enjoy your brief company in *Oyinbo* (the white man's) country,' my mother quipped on the eve of my departure. 'She has been on her own for six years and sure needs to feel her brother's hug. Are you sure you are coming back?'

I turned and looked sternly at my fussing mum as she crouched twiddling her Muslim prayer beads and chanting under her breath. 'Of course! I am only going for three months... we've been over this already, are you sure you really want me to go?'

'It's okay, my prince, let's not get into any arguments. There's just that look in your eyes.'

I have to confess that, as usual, she was right. Twenty-one years later I am still on my three-month holiday. Within a few days of stepping onto the British Isles, I had what we Pentecostals call 'an encounter' with God. The Holy Spirit spoke very vividly to me:

> Jonathan, you are not here by accident, you are here by divine design. You are here as part of my recruitment to this part of the world in preparation for the coming of my Son Jesus. Drop your agenda therefore and pick up my programme.

It was so clear and scary. So much so that I thought Jesus was coming back in 1994! It was so vivid and clear. I knew God was speaking to my heart. 'God, don't you think that's a bit too drastic and radical? Leave medicine? I have everything set up in Nigeria for my career. Can't I serve you as a medical doctor? How do I tell my dad? Wait a minute, how do I tell my mum?! Oh God, you are going to have to talk to her yourself!'

All these thoughts and more flooded through my mind as I pondered the depth of God's word to my heart. I was literally terrified of how my Islamic family would react to the news. I had barely recovered from the horrible experience of being excommunicated from our home by my father when I became a Christian five years earlier. For my parents, breeding the only doctor in the family anaesthetised the impact of having a Christian son within the Muslim community. Now even that joker was about to be lost.

Looking back, God has really been faithful. My entire family have become Christians, I met the love of my life, Abbiih, we have two lovely children Sam and Hanita, and for a while I was part of a thriving church called Glory House and deeply involved (in my own way) with Christian mission in the UK.

With hindsight, I now have a better panoramic view of a divine conspiracy behind the influx of exotic Christians into the UK. Heaven was responding to years of intercession to send help to strengthen flagging British congregations. The Lord Himself was building His church and Britain was reaping her harvest of overseas missionary work. Throughout the 1990s, in the back streets of Hackney, Leyton, Walthamstow, Lewisham, Brixton, Stratford, Finsbury Park, Islington and many other London inner-city districts, I saw churches birthed. Shop-front churches, home churches, warehouse churches, school churches, community-centre churches. Wherever there was ample space, a church was planted. In old buildings and new ones, in derelict cinemas or showrooms, in old cold and dusty church buildings, on housing estates and even in town halls. I thought it was normal.

African and Caribbean Christians overlapped in this era of frenzied church planting. Every other week we would receive glossy invitations to a church opening or a new building launch. It was much later that I began to find out that the established churches and Christian networks within the country were writing about the phenomenon of the black majority churches (BMCs). By the year

2000, statistical data reports were stating that 51 per cent of church attendees in London were black.

I know many fellow black Christians and even ministers who do not believe there are any significant indigenous Christian mission efforts within the UK. When I ask a black Pentecostal if she has ever attended Spring Harvest, the response is usually, 'Spring what?' or, 'Oh yeah I've heard of it… what do they do there?' When you ask a black Christian to name a 'good' white church or ministry within the capital they generally fumble for a name and may come up with Holy Trinity Brompton, Kensington Temple or the Alpha course.

The result is also similar in the reverse. Recently at a leaders' planning meeting with some core evangelical leaders, I asked if they had heard of the Redeemed Christian Church of God and their prayer nights called Festival of Life. They looked at me blankly and someone asked if I meant to say Festival of Light. I went on to tell them that the meetings are held two to three times a year in London with an average attendance of 15,000–17,000 per night. They really thought I was exaggerating. I was actually being conservative. Why do we have such a breakdown in communication across the cultural and ethnic divides?

Black and white Christians in Britain: The divide

I was almost in tears. I was angry, depressed and confused at the same time. It was November 2000 at the Evangelical Alliance (EA) Leadership Conference in Cardiff. Former London Bible College[21] icon Derek Tidball had just finished the morning Bible reading for the day. It was wonderful, but just added to my confusion. Where were all my black brothers? As I surveyed the approximately 98 per cent white congregation of more than 2,000 leaders, my thoughts travelled to Brighton four months earlier. I had been at a flagship conference within the black Christian community, a rich conglomeration of Caribbean and African Christians. The theme was

---

[21] Now the London School of Theology.

'Faith in the Future' and it was organised by the African and Caribbean Evangelical Alliance (ACEA).

At that wonderful convention in Brighton, with all its diversity of black Christian expression and culture, there I saw vividly the ominous black and white divide. I remember questioning my good friend the former EA General Director Joel Edwards, 'Why are we all meeting in camps?' was my blunt challenge.

In his usual amiable and uncle-like wise way, his reply was, 'That is one mountain a conference like this seeks to address and overcome. Our heart as an Alliance is to be a movement for change across the plurality of cultural and ethnic diversity within the church.'

I heckled him with more questions about why certain core white leaders were prominently absent, asking who had made the invitations, and a host of other barraging questions I can no longer recall.

As I travelled back to London from Cardiff, my mind was made up. I was on the phone to Joel at the earliest opportunity; 'Why is it that...?!' I let out a tirade of questions and protests. He was very patient with me and set out to calm me down and outline a course of action. This began a journey of discovery into the depth and breadth of the chasm between the white and black Christian communities in England.

I am not insinuating that all is doom and gloom with regard to interracial relationships in the church. I know many wonderful God-inspired ministries seeking to build bridges across ethnic borders. I do not claim to be an authority on race relations or cross-cultural dynamics within the church, but I do speak from personal experience.

At a National Leaders Conference and then at Spring Harvest 2004 in Minehead, I challenged the many white evangelical and charismatic leaders to adopt the spiritual sons that God Himself had brought to their shores. Reverend Terry Diggines, one of the founding fathers of the multicultural Newham Christian Fellowships (NCF), a central hub for the diversity of churches in east London, is a great model. A towering and swaggering man in his sixties, he has such a large heart. With open arms and a disarming humility of spirit he embraced me and the Glory House family that invaded the urban hamlet of Plaistow where he has lived for decades. 'You have brought fresh oil and fire from Africa. We need you guys here. Thank God you arrived!' he bellowed one summer afternoon while we had tea at his home. He meant every word, and that for me was the real miracle. I sat there looking quizzically at him. I could not help reflecting on whether, if I were in his shoes, I would be so enthused at a younger (and apparently more successful) minister in his prime in the arrival lounge while I was in the departure lounge. Without Terry Diggines and Joel Edwards, I would not have made it this far in the 'know-your-white-brother' venture from my church nest.

A call to unity

'Jonathan, this mission will impact London for Jesus!' I looked across the polyester cups strewn all over the wooden table at the man who had just frizzled the core of my bones with a vision larger than life itself. His hair was all over the place, dancing in black curls as he spoke animatedly. His shirt was a rainbow of colours and patterns that were speaking their own language. A bit of a distraction! His eyes were wide and childlike while his smile paradoxically seemed both on the verge of breaking into laughter and a frown at the same time. Yes, Mike Pilavachi, leader of the Soul Survivor movement, is an interesting character you don't forget in a hurry.

The launch of the Soul in the City Mission in 2003 was just weeks away at St Paul's Cathedral. Bringing 15,000 young people into London from across the United Kingdom and the world caught my imagination. As I arrived at the Leaders Reception in the massive crypt of the church, my worst fears were confirmed. I was back in Brighton and Cardiff (and many, many more meetings) as I saw a confluence of familiar faces and like colour. As I jumped and danced with more than 2,000 white youths singing Tim Hughes' inspired *Beautiful One*, the Holy Ghost came upon me and said, 'Strengthen this mission with your gift.'

'How in the world do you expect me to do that?' I retorted.

In His familiar unfazed and cool, quiet manner, above all the noise and shouting around me, above the ten-foot blaring speakers and clanging cymbals, He whispered loud in my heart, 'Get involved, Jonathan.'

My involvement in the Soul in the City mission was primarily to see souls saved and the church healed of its racial chasms, and more than 670 churches registered. My hope to far exceed the 1,000 mark was then fulfilled. Within the months of my participation, I saw Anglican vicars teaming up with young Pentecostals, and long-standing rifts between some church leaders terminated as they came together to plan a project. Many churches discovered each other, just like Mungo Park discovered the Nile that had always been there. A group of churches planned a beauty parlour project for young Asian girls as an outreach to the Islamic and Hindu community around them. All over London Anglican, Independent, Methodist, Pentecostal, Baptist, Catholic and United Reformed Churches linked up with each other. This definitely put a smile on God's face and got angels doing the salsa!

> My prayer is not for them alone. I pray also for those who will believe in me through their message, that all of them may be one, Father, just as you are in me and I am in you. May they also be in us so that the world may believe that you have sent me. I have given them the glory that you gave me, that they may be one as we are one. (John 17:20-22)

I leave you with one little assignment. As a Christian, lay person, minister, pastor or bishop, please make some good friends with those outside your cultural or ethnic identity. Get to know their homes, the names of their children, eat with them and make them part of your life. Jesus said, 'And if you greet only your own people, what are you doing more than others?' (Matthew 5:47).

A call to prayer: vision for the UK church

> I urge, then, first of all, that petitions, prayers, intercession and thanksgiving be made for all people – for kings and all those in authority, that we may live peaceful and quiet lives in all godliness and holiness ... I want the men everywhere [in Britain] to pray, lifting up holy hands without anger or disputing. (1 Timothy 2:1,8)

In the year 2005 I had a repeated vision of something I first saw in 1991. It was clearer and came with its own insight and application. Before stating what I saw, I would like to present two other scenes that I was given by the Lord, in 1992 and 1997.

Visions, dreams, trances and prophetic revelations are all very biblical and can be experienced by any Christian as a result of gifts given by the Holy Spirit or as chosen by the Lord. Saint Peter quoted from the book of Joel on the Day of Pentecost when he said:

> In the last days, God says, I will pour out my Spirit on all people. Your sons and daughters will prophesy, your young men will see visions, your old men will dream dreams. Even on my servants, both men and women, I will pour out my Spirit in those days, and they will prophesy. (Acts 2:17-18)

The Old and New Testaments are replete with incidences and stories of people having divinely inspired epiphanies resulting in God communicating a message with a purpose. God seems to have chosen to speak to me many times through dreams and visions, right from the very first day I encountered Jesus as my Saviour. With this in mind, let me tell you what I saw.

The road to Wembley
The first vision was thousands of people who looked like Christians worshipping and praying at Wembley Stadium. At that time (1992), I had never been to the stadium, but had watched matches on TV. However, the stadium I saw was more modern and different from

the Wembley Stadium I had seen. It was a different stadium, but in the experience I knew that it was definitely Wembley.

Everybody was there to celebrate and pray, and the large podium that had been erected was all set and ready, but empty. We all seemed to be waiting for someone to come to the microphone. All the Christian profiled leaders, speakers and many others were there but all were stationary, looking at the microphone. As I looked on and waited, the Lord said to my heart, 'Jonathan, when my people gather in unity, I am the one that speaks' – 'For where two or three are gathered *together* in my name, there am I in the midst of them' (Matthew 18:20, KJV, italics added).

I recorded the vision in my heart and rehearsed it to a number of leaders I knew at that time, but I didn't know what was required of me, so l prayed about it, prayed into unity in the Body of Christ, and later shelved it. Nevertheless, I did not forget it.

The Pied Piper

The second vision I experienced was later in the 1990s. I saw hundreds of thousands of people, probably more than a million, streaming out from nightclubs, libraries, homes, streets, pubs, workplaces, factories, churches, mosques, temples, city centres… everywhere. Some were well dressed; others looked as though they were homeless. Their hairstyles were of all shapes, shades and styles. The striking thing was that they were all *teenagers*!

It looked like a scene from the Pied Piper fable with a Stephen King eerie twist as they all seemed to be responding to a certain call or sound. They had a dreamy look on their faces but their brows were furrowed with determination and purpose. They were teenagers from all cultural groups and nationalities, although the overwhelming majority were Caucasian Brits. They poured onto the empty streets and filled the dual carriage way as far as my eyes could see. It looked like the M1 motorway.

I came out of the frame, dream or vision shouting in my mind, 'They are here! They are all here!' I suddenly *knew* that Britain was a Christian nation and I heard the Lord say, 'When I call, my sheep hear my voice, respond and obey' (see John 10:11-16). The meaning of the vision was thousands or perhaps millions of young Britons responding to God, but this is in sharp contrast with this present hedonistic, self-serving and liberal society.

As a British-born Nigerian, saved from Islam and called as a missionary to Great Britain, I see a Western world that is quite confused. One minute we are reducing the age of consent for having sex, and the very next we are banning smoking while reclassifying cannabis. The legal age of consent to have an abortion is lower than that for having sex! We preach a message of political correctness but want to remove the traditional Christian values that have formed the foundation stones of current British society's norms and laws. In the name of tolerance, Britain is in danger of losing her identity.

I stepped into 2006 with an overwhelming burden to act as a catalyst to call the city in which I live – London – to prayer. This call, however, is to the whole nation. We need to get on our knees before God or we will kneel before an anti-Christian state. This call is for the church to regain her job description of intercession and prayer with fasting for the world:

> If my people, who are called by my name, will humble themselves and pray and seek my face and turn from their wicked ways, then I will hear from heaven, and I will forgive their sin and will heal their land. (2 Chronicles 7:14)

The third reel
In the third vision, the Lord gave me a simple illustration of joining the dots. I saw what looked like a map of Britain with the location of *all* the churches (in homes, factories, shops, historic buildings or converted warehouses) linked together. Each church was praying the same prayer as the next and there was some kind of cord or connection joining each church with the others. I clearly saw each church as groups of people or congregations praying together. *Each church looked like a light bulb.* Then, as the people continued to pray, all the churches lit up as individual lights, and it seemed that the whole country was covered in lights, like a Christmas tree! I saw the words *light* and *healing* emblazoned across the map of the UK. When the church begins to pray in unity, light and healing will come to the British Isles in increasing measure.

Six years ago I was a catalyst for consistent united prayer in the borough of Newham. We have been praying together every week since. That area of London is undergoing transformation in spiritual, social, financial and infrastructural terms. Our vision is to cover the whole borough in prayer. I strongly believe we need to come together in prayer: '… they were all with one accord in one place' (Acts 2:1, KJV).

The call

In June 2006, I issued a call for united prayers, for church leaders and people in the pews to pray for our communities, cities, counties and country as a whole. I challenged Christians to be a catalyst wherever they were and to call the churches and Christians in their areas together to pray on the Day of Pentecost, Sunday 4th June 2006. This invitation was honoured, and Christians in this country took on the challenge.

Pentecost is celebrated by the church all over the world. The root of Pentecost (Acts 2) is unity in prayer and worship. Could Britain celebrate this festival in the true spirit of its genesis? On 20th February 2006, a number of leaders across the Christian streams got together in one of the key churches in London and left with a united mandate to have a gathering that year linked in to the Global Day of Prayer (which had started in South Africa in 2001). The result of that was the first Global Day of Prayer London event at Westminster Chapel on 4th June 2006. Those in attendance were church leaders from different denominations, youth workers, business leaders, MPs, civic leaders, community leaders and Christians from different church traditions. The capital's Christian leadership converged in one place on this day to establish the unity of the church and to pray for the city and the nation. We supplicated, interceded and offered up thanksgiving to the Father through the Son in the Spirit.

This event was supported by Charismatic Catholics, evangelicals, Pentecostals, Anglicans, black majority churches, Baptists, Methodists and multi-ethnic church communities all over London. All the major denominations, independent churches and networks were linked together through this prayer gathering. That Pentecost Sunday witnessed united prayers with fasting in local churches across the capital as congregations prayed the same prayer of thanksgiving, supplication and intercession in various styles and liturgies. Some areas, such as Southwark and Newham, planned large celebrations in their local parks.

The year 2007 saw Christians in the capital gathered together at West Ham's Upton Park football stadium, praying and worshipping together in unity. There were also prayer gatherings and events in all of the 32 boroughs in London, and in the City of London. Pentecost day in May 2008 saw another gathering of Christians in this nation at Millwall stadium. There was also a prayer relay in all of London's 32 boroughs focusing on the increase in gun and knife crime in the capital.

In 2009, the prayer vision took a different direction as there was no big stadium event. Instead, what took place was prayer gatherings and events in all of the 32 boroughs in London, the City of London and four home counties. In all, there were about 50 different praying centres all over the UK. This was partly to demonstrate to people that prayer is not about the numbers or big events.

In 2010, the prayer event went back to West Ham's stadium as Christians from all over the nation gathered to pray for our nation and its government. The 500 Days of Prayer also started in August 2010 and ended in December 2011, with television broadcasts and radio programmes accompanying the event.

The year 2011 saw the first fulfilment of the vision for Wembley Stadium as church leaders, MPs, youth leaders, community leaders, business leaders and civic leaders all gathered to pray at a leaders' reception.

The vision for Wembley was fulfilled on 29th September 2012. This event broke down all barriers: it was ecumenical, intergenerational and multicultural in participation and attendance. It brought together various streams and networks of churches from all across the UK. An official count of 32,649 Christians from all over Britain gathered together to pray, repent and celebrate Jesus at Wembley stadium. The day started with about 1,500 church leaders gathering at the leaders' reception to pray and fellowship together, and also to be inspired about fresh mission initiatives developing across the UK. The reception was followed by the National Day of Prayer (NDOP). This was an inspiring event as Christians prayed for church unity in this country, for youth crime to reduce, for children in poverty all over the world and for the UK government. The event also saw the profiling of initiatives such as Crossing London 2013, Hope 2014, Tearfund relief projects in poorer parts of the world and the children's Christmas shoebox initiative Operation Christmas Child by Samaritan's Purse. The event was not about profiling one church leader, as different denominational leaders and church organisations led prayers. This was in faithfulness to the vision given 20 years ago; it was about celebrating Jesus!

Due to an overwhelming response and feedback from various regions and places around the British Isles, the next stage of the vision of the NDOP is to partner with churches all around the country to continue to pray for the UK. This prayer initiative is known as the Join the Dots Tour and will see NDOP going all over the country partnering and working alongside existing prayer initiatives. This initiative came about through my speaking engagements, which ranged from personal opportunities to national conferences and church engagement. The vision was communicated to about 150 partners and church leaders at the NDOP reception at Portcullis House, Houses of Parliament, in February 2013. The meeting was hosted by Gary Streeter MP, Stephen Timms MP and David Burrowes MP, all from the All Party Parliamentary Group Christians in Parliament. Leaders from a number of streams and networks across the country came together to take the vision of the National Day of Prayer and Worship forward into a new season. The celebration really saw the best of the church at prayer!

We see this vision as the legacy of the National Day of Prayer that took place at Wembley. We have some lovely partnerships in place with church denominations and many regional networks and organisations including the World Prayer Centre, Saltbox, Neighbourhood Prayer Network, Light in the Land, Urban Saints, United Christian Broadcasting (UCB) and many others. There is an increasing sense of gathering in unity to bring tens of thousands of Christians together and inspire them to unite, pray and share their faith within their own localities. In the autumn of 2013 we are also believing God that a national event will take place in the north of the UK.

Reflections

Jonathan Oloyede's story is significant on several points. First, he was from a strong Islamic background in Nigeria. This is important as I think it gave him the necessary discipline and devotion needed in the place of prayer, which characterise his ministry. This reveals how God prepares us even before we realise, and uses experiences from our past to train us for what He is calling us to do. Against his parents' wishes and family dream and prestige, Jonathan became a Christian and would later abandon practising as a medical doctor to answer God's call. For an average Nigerian family that prides itself in terms of its children's professional career achievements, this is very costly and painful. But it is this sacrifice that defines Jonathan's call to Britain and his ministry here. Jonathan also shares how God worked in his family's life so that in time they came to understand and support his decisions, and to find faith in Jesus for themselves.

Jonathan was not sent to Britain by a church or missionary organisation in Nigeria, but by God Himself. His conviction that God has called him as a missionary to Britain has driven him to get involved in several mission initiatives and organisations such as Soul in the City, the Evangelical Alliance, More than Gold, Spring Harvest and Soul Survivor. It was the same conviction that led him to leave his former church, Glory House, and start a new one that would reflect the cultural diversity that we experience in London.

He is obviously passionate about the biblical call to unity and saddened at the division he sees in many areas of the church in the UK. Like the great pioneer of mission, Philip Mohabir, Jonathan has sought and worked hard to unite black and white Christians in the UK. He has done this through united prayer, reminding the UK church of the need to seek God's face in humility and prayer. This is the strength and significance of the Global and National Day of Prayer initiatives. The NDOP event held in Wembley in 2012 has also challenged those who say that large gatherings cannot happen in the UK these days. Anyone who attended the event at Wembley, as I did, would no longer doubt what God can do!

It is also encouraging to read Jonathan's testimony of how the visions God spoke to him almost two decades ago are now being fulfilled, encouraging us to stand firm and have faith that what God has said He will do will come to pass.

Chapter Five
Multicultural churches in Britain:
the journey to Crofton Park Baptist Church
Israel Olofinjna

Introduction

In this chapter I want to explore the rise of multicultural Britain, and ask whether the Windrush generation[22] was in fact the beginning of multiracial Britain. Attention will be given to the history and growth of black majority churches through the lens of African-led congregations. What factors led to the formation of black majority churches, and what is their relationship with British historic churches? I will also consider the significance of multicultural churches, reflecting on my own journey as an African immigrant sent to plant a Nigerian Pentecostal church in Britain, but ending up as the pastor of a multicultural church in south-east London (Crofton Park Baptist Church). Other issues explored include the challenges of a multicultural congregation and the significance of a multicultural church in a multiracial society such as Britain.

It is worth clarifying some terms before proceeding. The term 'multiculturalism' is very difficult to define as it depends on who is using it and for what purpose. In addition, it has become more problematic due to government policies shaping state multiculturalism. An example is the British government's call for the end of multiculturalism because it has failed to integrate people.

Multiculturalism is a word that is often associated with the rhetoric of political correctness. People are therefore wary of using

---

[22] The Windrush generation is an expression used to describe the migration of Caribbean people to Britain from 1948 to the 1960s. SS Empire Windrush was the name of the ship that carried about 492 Caribbean people on 22nd June 1948, docking at Tilbury, London. The migration of the Caribbean people was a result of the invitation that the British government extended to them in order to help rebuild Britain after the devastation of the Second World War.

the term, and prefer to use other words such as 'cultural diversity'. The attempt here to define multiculturalism is not to solve the problems associated with the term, but is for the purpose of a working definition in this chapter. Multiculturalism is here defined as the coexistence and meaningful engagement of different ethnicities (biological and cultural differences) and cultures (that which is transmittable and accumulative through society and not by genes). Depending on several factors, some of which will be explored below, multiculturalism in practice can lead to a) integration: mutual coexistence, engagement and equality of host and minority cultures; b) assimilation: the absorption of minority cultures into the host culture; or c) separation: the existence of cultures without meaningful interaction and engagement.

Historical development of multicultural Britain

There is a general assumption, both in public and political rhetoric, that Britain became multiracial with the arrival of Caribbean immigrants in the 1940s. In political discourse, this is perpetuated by the myth that pure white Britishness needs to be preserved in the face of immigration. The National Front formed in 1967, and one of its chief aims was to prevent people migrating to Britain, especially people of colour. Its leaders, who had been involved in Nazi activities, were keen supporters of Hitler.[23] It is no surprise, then, that they embraced an ideology of nationalism that was rooted in the science of 'racial purity'. The British National Party (BNP) was founded in 1982, and though less aggressive and overt in their policies, they continued the campaign to protect white Britishness. From 2001, New Labour campaigned for a national story of Britishness and its values in their efforts to tackle terrorism and reduce immigration. This Britishness was couched in the language of integration. The coalition government, since coming to power in 2010, appears to have continued in Labour's footsteps, pronouncing

---

[23] Stott, John (1999), *Issues Facing Christians Today*, London, Harper Collins, p.249.

an end to state multiculturalism. This is evident in recent comments made by the Secretary of State for Communities and Local Government, Mr Eric Pickles, who has pledged to end the era of multiculturalism, arguing that Britain needs community cohesion around British values and identity.[24] Therefore, while the National Front and BNP wanted to preserve white Britishness, the Labour and Conservative parties are also promoting the preservation of a British national identity. In order to have a British national identity that can be integrated with, it is considered necessary to have a national story. It is interesting to observe that in 2012 alone, the BBC and Channel Four televised three documentaries that appeared to be telling a national story: *Empire* and *God Made the English* produced by the BBC, and *Make Bradford British* by Channel Four.

How, then, is Britishness perceived by the general public? There is a normative idea among the public that to be British, or particularly to be English, is to be white. This is demonstrated through many white British attitudes that do not accept any non-white people as British. Therefore, if your ethnicity is Asian British or black British, you are rejected as not being British. An example of this attitude was revealed during the Channel Four documentary *Make Bradford British*[25] in which an Asian British lady was criticised by white British people in a pub. The criticism, which reduced her to tears, centred on questioning her identity as a British Pakistani Muslim. The white British simply told her that she was not British because she was a Muslim from a Pakistani background. If the current political language on integration is centred on a British national identity and story, and the public understanding of Britishness means whiteness, the question is, what is this Britishness? Or to put it another way, is Britishness monocultural or multicultural?

The place we know today as Britain has its foundations in mixed cultures, therefore cultural diversity is nothing new here. While little

---

[24] http://www.dailymail.co.uk/news/article-2104049/Eric-Pickles-signals-end-multiculturalism-says-Tories-stand-majority.html?ITO=google_news_rss_feed (accessed 15 August 2013).
[25] *Make Bradford British*, Channel 4 documentary aired on 8th March 2012.

is known about the first people who inhabited these islands, we do know that the Celts (people originally descended from dwellers on the Russian steppes) arrived at these shores around the first millennium BC.[26] The people spoke the Celtic dialect which is still used today in some parts of Wales, Scotland and Ireland. They had a sophisticated culture and economy and merged with the original population.

In the first century AD, Celtic Britain, south of Hadrian's Wall, was ruled by the Roman Empire. The Roman invasion and subsequent conquest began with Julius Caesar's visit around 55 BC. The Romans ruled Britannia for a total of 400 years, after which its Empire declined due to the Barbarians' invasion. At this time, in the fifth century AD, new Germanic tribes from northern Europe invaded Britain. These warring tribes came from what is known today as northern Germany, southern Denmark and the northern part of the Netherlands, and were the Angles, Saxons, Jutes and Frisians.[27] Venerable Bede, in his *Ecclesiastical History of the English People*, recorded how the Angles, Saxons and Jutes were invited by the British people to come and fight the Romans on their behalf, but they ended up conquering Britain itself.[28] Their conquest of Britain led to a synthesis of culture and language known as Anglo-Saxon.

In the eighth and ninth centuries AD, fresh invasions and migrants came from Scandinavia: the Vikings of Denmark and Norway. This led to further mixed cultures as the Norse culture was introduced. Around AD 1066 there was another invasion, this time by the Normans. This invasion was led by the popular William, Duke of Normandy (part of France today), also known as William the Conqueror. The Norman culture, language and customs were therefore introduced, and this had a huge influence on the British population.

One of William the Conqueror's actions when he reigned was the encouragement of large Jewish settlements in Britain. He allowed

---

[26] *Roots of the Future*, (1997), Commission for Racial Equality, London, p.7.
[27] Ibid., p.7.
[28] Bede (2008), The *Ecclesiastical History of the English People*, Oxford, Oxford University Press, pp.26-27.

Jews from France to settle, offering them royal protection. This allowed for an influx of Jews so that by the thirteenth century there were Jewish populations in 27 cities, including London.

Jews were not the only migrants to Britain during the early Middle Ages; other Europeans such as Germans and Italians arrived as merchants or simply visitors. The Reformation started by Martin Luther, Ulrich Zwingli, John Calvin and others led to religious wars in Europe which resulted in thousands of highly skilled Protestant refugees fleeing to Britain for protection. Not everyone welcomed these refugees; some cried 'Tottenham is turned Flemish' and Bermondsey was called 'Petty Burgundy'.[29]

The eighteenth century witnessed the rise of the black population in Britain. This was due to the evil and inhumane trade known as the trans-Atlantic slave trade, or triangular trade, which had begun in the fifteenth century. This trade was well established by the eighteenth century and resulted in a population of about 15,000 Africans in London by the year 1700.

While African slaves were serving in British society in the middle of the eighteenth century, Germans also came and settled in Britain. Many were professionals equipped with financial and industrial skills, and they contributed to Britain's industrial and economic development. By 1914, the German population in Britain had risen to about 40,000. Later, a mass migration of Russians and Polish Jews occurred, following mass unemployment after the Great Depression of 1929. Many also arrived as a result of persecution in communist regimes. Finally, the post-war years saw Caribbean people and those from European countries coming to Britain in response to invitations to come and rebuild the country after the devastation of the Second World War. Workers were also recruited from India, Pakistan and Bangladesh. The end of colonialism in African countries also witnessed a great number of African diplomats and students coming to settle in Britain from the 1960s.

This quick survey is to demonstrate that what we know today as Britain has been multicultural since its origins. Britain itself was, in fact, formed in the 1707 union of Scotland and England, later

---

[29] *Roots of the Future*, p.13.

extended to the Welsh and Irish, and is therefore multicultural in its very essence, given that it is a combination of distinct nations.

Why are multicultural churches important in Britain?

Having surveyed the historical development of multiracial and multicultural Britain, I now want to discuss the significance in society of multicultural churches. In order to do this, my discussion will start with state multiculturalism and its weaknesses. Modern multicultural Britain (that is, since the 1940s) has given rise to two main political discourses. The first is that of those on the right wing of British politics whose contention is that cultural diversity is a threat to national identity and security. They have argued that an over-tolerance of multiculturalism has allowed immigrants to segregate rather than integrate. They therefore call for assimilation – the absorption and conformity of all other cultures into the British culture, identity and values. Extreme versions of this ideology would be the National Front and the BNP.

The second political discourse is that of the liberals and those on the centre-left who advocate for cultural diversity. The kind of multiculturalism they have historically fought for can be summed up in former Home Secretary Roy Jenkins' famous 1966 definition of integration as 'equal opportunity accompanied by cultural diversity in an atmosphere of mutual tolerance'.[30] They have consciously fought against assimilation in favour of such a model of integration.

However, this type of 'integration' is changing, giving way to a new integration paradigm that, while still campaigning for equal opportunities, in fact has assimilation as its objective. Among the reasons for this change were the events of 11th September 2001 in New York and the later 7th July 2005 bombings in London by home-grown perpetrators,[31] as well as the race riots that took place in

---

[30] *Racism and the State (2007)*, Race and Class Volume 48 # 4, Institute of Race Relations, London, p.27.

[31] The brutal murder of Lee Rigby on the afternoon of 22nd May 2013 in Woolwich by two black Islamist extremist British men has also highlighted

Bradford, Burnley and Oldham in 2001.[32] From around that period, liberals and those on the centre-left advocated community cohesion as a form of integration.[33] Therefore, those on the right now have allies from the liberals and centre-left who all agree that multiculturalism must be 'managed'.

One extension of this is the argument that managed migration is needed at our borders as a way of combating terrorism, leading to measures such as the increased use of surveillance technologies, immigration caps, visa restrictions, deportations and detentions, undermining fundamental human rights. The rhetoric of fighting terrorism comes under the guise of the 'war on terror', and this has led to the mistreatment and stigmatisation of immigrants coming from Islamic countries and cultures. The language of 'illegal' or 'bogus' immigrants generally seems to apply only to non-white immigrants – white Australians, South Africans and New Zealanders being exempt –[34] and is one of the new expressions of institutional racism (this language is often not applied to British citizens who are working illegally, for example in Australia).[35] The British cry is that immigrants are not integrating; therefore the multicultural agenda has failed. However, the question is, why are immigrants not mixing?

---

the notion of home-grown perpetrators, forcing questions of integration, race and religion back to the fore of public discourse.

[32] *Racism and the State,* pp.26 and 78.

[33] Community cohesion is hereby defined as the government's attempt to bring togetherness into a given community through funding local projects that will bond people of different ethnicities, religions and cultures.

[34] Over the past ten years there has been a steady migration of people from Eastern European countries such as Poland, Romania and Bulgaria in the last decade. While the term 'illegal' has not been applied to them because their countries are part of the European Union (EU), general attitudes towards them in certain quarters have been hostile as well, and it will be interesting to see a comparative study of the experiences of these non-Commonwealth 'white immigrants' with those of the non-whites described here.

[35] *Racism and the State,* p.28.

Using immigrants as scapegoats for the failure of multiculturalism or accusing them of not integrating is just one side of the story; the other side is to recognise and deal with the issues of institutional and personal racism that I think still exist in British society today. Britain likes to think that it is post-racial, that it has wrestled with racism and expunged it. However, the truth is that racism still exists in our society. One way to illustrate this is what is known as 'white flight',[36] a pattern of migration that sees white families moving out of a neighbourhood as non-white immigrants move in. This can be applied to youth clubs, schools, pubs, gyms and churches. A good example of white flight is what has happened in Peckham. Peckham used to be almost entirely white in the early 1960s. However, now it is full of non-white immigrants from different parts of the world. Similarly, Brixton and Southall used to be predominantly white. How are the incoming blacks, Asians or South Americans supposed to integrate if the white British are not there to mix with them?

Community cohesion is attempting to integrate immigrants, but it must also address the issue of racism. Institutional racism still exists within British society's structures, such as the police. The latest evidence from the Stephen Lawrence enquiry is a case in point. Despite the Macpherson report in 1999 into the death of the south London teenager and its clear conclusion of institutional racism as a cause, the recommendations were not fully implemented.[37] On the one hand, the recommendations led to the amending of the Race Relation Acts and required national bodies such as the police and NHS to examine the racism within their institutions. However, on the other hand, the recommendations were undermined by the Labour Party's new language of integration that was gaining ground, and policies such as restrictive immigration controls and detention centres.

Another sign of institutional racism is the recent cry of Stephen Lawrence's brother, Stuart Lawrence, against the stop-and-search

---

[36] 'White flight' is not always an evidence of racism and can be caused by varied socio-economic and cultural factors.
[37] *Racism and the State*, pp.34-35.

tactics of the Metropolitan Police. Stuart Lawrence says that he has been stopped about 25 times simply because of his skin colour. He is planning to take legal action and campaign against such racial injustice.[38] If racism is still a menace in our society, at both a personal and national level, what is the role of the church in combating this?

To answer this question, we have to begin by surveying the history of black majority churches (BMCs). The start of BMCs in Britain is usually traced back to the 1940s, although evidence suggests that there were a number of BMCs in Britain before this time. The first BMC in the UK was a Pentecostal church by the name of Sumner Road Chapel. This church was started in Peckham in around 1906 by Rev Thomas Kwame Brem-Wilson (1855–1929), a Ghanaian businessman.[39] The church later became affiliated with the Assemblies of God Britain in 1939 and is today known as Sureway International Ministries, relocated to Herne Hill in south London. Another BMC led by a Nigerian, Daniels Ekarte (1890s–1964), started in 1931 in Toxteth, Liverpool. The name of the church was African Churches Missions (ACM).

The next phase of church planting in the history of BMCs in Britain was the start of the Caribbean churches. These churches include Calvary Church of God in Christ (1948), Church of God in Christ (1952), Church of God of Prophecy (1953), New Testament Church of God (1953), Church of our Lord Jesus Christ of the Apostolic Faith (1957), Wesleyan Holiness Church (1958), Church of the First Born (1958), and New Testament Assembly (1961). Many of these churches were plants of church denominations already in existence in the Caribbean, while others originated in the UK, such as the Bethel United Church of Jesus Christ (1955). There are several

---

[38] http://www.independent.co.uk/news/uk/home-news/stephen-lawrences-brother-to-sue-met-for-discrimination-8444082.html (accessed January 2013).

[39] Cartwright, Desmond (2007), 'Black Pentecostal Churches in Britain' in *Journal of European Pentecostal Theology Association*, Vol 23, No 2 and http://glorymag.blogspot.co.uk/2011/04/sureway-international-christian.html (accessed July 2013).

reasons why these churches started. While racism and exclusion from historic churches played a key role in their establishment, it must be mentioned that this was not the entire picture. Dr Joe Aldred, an ecumenist and black theologian, argues that mission was also a priority among Caribbean immigrants and that they were actually accepted in some mainstream churches.[40] The Caribbean churches brought an energy and dynamism to British Christianity at a time when traditional Christianity was declining.[41]

The 1960s saw African nations gain independence from their colonial masters. This, coupled with the fact that there were no border restrictions for immigrants from the British Commonwealth, led to Africans settling in different parts of Britain as students, tourists and diplomats. Many came with their religion, but as they began to settle down they realised firstly that historic churches were largely unwelcoming. Many black people were refused entry and rejected when they approached British historic churches. Father Olu Abiola's story is a case to illustrate this. He came to Britain as an Anglican priest in the 1950s with the hope that he could be part of the Church of England. To his amazement, he was shown the way out.

Second, the majority of African immigrants found traditional British Christianity very cold compared to the vibrancy of their home churches.

Lastly, the educational, social, economic and financial needs of African and Caribbean people were not met by the British historic churches.

These factors, combined with a passion for mission, led to another wave of church plants known as African churches or African Initiated Churches (AICs). The Church of the Lord Aladura was the first of these churches to be planted and was started by the late Apostle Adejobi in south London in 1964. It was followed by

---

[40] Aldred, J. D. (2005), *Respect*, Werrington, Peterborough, Epworth Publishers, pp.80-90.
[41] Hill, Clifford (1971), *Black Churches: West Indian and African Sects in Britain*, London, Community and Race Relations Unit of the British Council of Churches, p.3.

Cherubim and Seraphim Church (C&S) in 1965 and Celestial Church of Christ (CCC) in 1967. Aladura International Church was founded by Father Olu Abiola in 1970 as an independent AIC. Christ Apostolic Church (CAC) Mount Bethel was founded in London in 1974 by Apostle Ayo Omideyi, with another Christ Apostolic Church (CAC) founded in 1976.

All the above churches (except for Father Abiola's church) had their mother church in Nigeria. Musama Disco Christo Church (MDCC), a Ghanaian AIC, also began in Britain around 1980.

The 1980s and 90s witnessed an explosion and proliferation of African Pentecostal churches in Britain. While some of these were church plants from mother churches back in Africa, the majority were independent churches with a mission to start churches in Europe. These churches are referred to as Newer Pentecostal Churches (NPCs) because they are new compared to Classic Pentecostal Churches.

This brief survey of the historical development of BMCs reveals that racial discrimination had a part to play in the founding of these churches.

White flight has also been an issue in the church. This has happened in cases where a black minister or church leader has started pastoring a British historic church such as a Baptist, Anglican, Catholic, United Reformed or Methodist church. As a result, some white members of the congregations have left these churches, while the number of black Christians has increased. This was the case at Custom House Baptist Church (started in 1906), now led by Rev Tade Agbesanwa. Before he started pastoring the church it was white majority; however, after being under his leadership for some time, the church gradually became a BMC. There are still white people there but they are in the minority.

Another way white flight occurs in a church context is when black Christians start attending a white majority church. Over time, the dynamic can change so that the church becomes a BMC, or a multicultural church with whites in the minority. This was the case at Greenford Baptist Church led by Rev David Wise. What is fascinating is the fact that David is white British, but this was not sufficient to stop white flight. David had a vision of a multicultural church when he started leading there in 1987. This changed the church from white majority to a multicultural church with black Christians in the majority.

White flight and the human propensity of 'relating with our own', among other factors, have led to different sections of society having their own churches. This means that we now have in Britain black majority churches, white majority churches (although we must remember that white is no more a singular ethnic category than black is), Hispanic churches, Portuguese-speaking churches, Spanish-speaking churches, Tamil churches, Korean churches, Chinese churches, Indian churches, Hungarian churches, and the list goes on. These polarisations and divisions in the church mirror what is happening in our society, as we have black communities, Asian communities, South American communities, white communities, Jewish communities and so on. However, in the midst of these cultural and ethnic divisions, both in society and the church, we also have churches that are creating an alternative space for the multicultural diverse people of God. These multicultural churches are counter cultural and kingdom oriented, breaking down the artificial barriers that try to separate us. These barriers include race, culture, ethnicity, gender, class, disability and age.

These multiculturally diverse churches are what Bruce Milne refers to in his book, *Dynamic Diversity*, as the 'New Humanity Church': a new kind of community of God's people that transcends any form of division.[42] Milne takes the term 'New Humanity' from Ephesians 2:15 (TNIV translation) where Paul talks about Christ's work on the cross breaking down the barriers between Jews and Gentiles. In Ephesians 2:11-22 Paul talks about how Christ's work on the cross reconciled us back to God (a vertical relationship with God), and that he also pulled down the wall that divides us as humans (horizontal relationships with our neighbours).

In the time of Paul and the other apostles, this wall of division would have been the hostilities that existed among different ethnic communities such as those that existed between Jews and

---

[42]Bruce Milne (2006), *Dynamic Diversity: The New Humanity Church for Today and Tomorrow*, Nottingham, Intervarsity Press, pp.15-16.

Samaritans, Jews and Gentiles, Romans and Barbarians, Greeks and non-Greeks and men and women. Some of the Jewish laws in the Old Testament, while meant to be kept as identity markers for the Israelites, were also used to ensure separation from other ethnic groups. Some of these divisions can be seen in areas such as the dietary laws and circumcision (see Acts 10 and 15). The various separations in Herod's Temple were a mirror of what was going on in their society. The divisions in the Temple included the Holy Place for only the High Priest, the Court of the Priest for other priests, the Court of Israel for only Israelite men, the Court of Women for Israelite women and the Court of the Gentiles for everyone who was not a Jew. These various separations were taken seriously: if a Gentile dared to enter the Court of Israel it would have been at the cost of his or her life. To illustrate this, when Paul was arrested, one of the accusations brought against him was that he brought Greeks into the Temple area (Acts 21:27-29). Paul's theology was that Christ's death brought an end to these artificial segregations. He went further to say that this was why he had been chosen by God to be an apostle to the Gentiles (Ephesians 3:1-7).

Paul's theology of unity in diversity is what these multiculturally diverse churches are putting into practice. They are therefore significant because, despite the fact that Britain is a multicultural society, the reality is that racism and classism still exist within both society and the church.

The dynamics and challenges of a multiculturally diverse church: case study of Crofton Park Baptist Church

I left the shores of my country on 1st October 2004. It was Nigerian Independence Day and yet here I was travelling to 'the Mother Country'. The purpose of my journey was twofold: first, it was to do a postgraduate degree in theology, and secondly it was to start a Pentecostal church/ministry in the UK.

My church back in Nigeria (Fountain of Grace Chapel, Ibadan) was a newer Pentecostal Church founded in 1992. I became a member of this church in December 1995 when I gave my heart to the Lord at the watchnight service organised by the church. However, I must mention that my spiritual journey started with my family. I was born into what would be regarded as a Christian family and attended my mother's church, an African Instituted Church (Cherubim and Seraphim) when I was a child. One good thing that came out of attending this church was that it helped prepare me spiritually for what I would be doing later. For some reason the church gave me the task to carry the cross before the preacher went on to deliver his sermon (this was part of the tradition of this church). I did not really like this, but on reflection it was almost like a sign that I was going to be a preacher one day. Shortly after committing my life to the Lord I became a youth leader and a house group leader at Fountain of Grace Chapel. I attended the Bible college founded by the church (Grace Bible Institute) in 1997 and graduated in 1998. I was involved in three church-planting projects, one of them being part of the Bible college qualification. After graduating from there I furthered my theological studies by doing a BA Honours degree in Religious Studies at the University of Ibadan from 1999 to 2003.

During my undergraduate days I was actively involved with the Christian Union, popularly known as IVCU (Ibadan Varsity Christian Union). This fellowship, which dates back to the 1960s, is renowned in West Africa for its evangelical heritage. One of its legacies is that over the years it has trained and developed church leaders with integrity and character in Nigeria and beyond. Among such is W. F. Kumuyi, the founder of Deeper Life Bible Church. Some of the activities I was involved with at IVCU included mission, pastoral oversight, teaching, youth mentoring, schools work and prayer ministry.

While studying I was also actively involved in organising academic seminars in my department, exploring the subject of Nigerian church history.

After completing my studies I started working in the Fountain of Grace Chapel office. My role involved assisting the pastors, healing ministry and teaching and discipling the youth of the church. I did this for a period of six months before travelling to the UK.

Over the years, members of Fountain of Grace Chapel had travelled and settled down in the UK, therefore a part of my task when I came to Britain in 2004 was to gather these members and start a church. I was very excited about this venture and embraced it with enthusiasm. However, on arrival, and after observing the church scene in the UK, I discovered that there were many Nigerian churches that had not managed to attract white British indigenes. This was for many reasons, including that many of these churches did not know how to engage in cross-cultural missions. Convinced that something had to be done differently, I decided to abandon the church plant and join an existing British historic church. This was not an easy decision, but it was one I felt was needed if I was to truly be a missionary to Britain. My pastor was initially upset, understandably, but later understood and supported my decision.

I therefore started attending Crofton Park Baptist Church in south-east London. Crofton Park is a multicultural church that draws people from white British, African and African Caribbean heritage. The church has a history of welcoming ethnic minorities which stretches back to the 1960s when it welcomed Caribbean families at a time when many historic churches closed their doors to them. In 1987, the church hosted Rev Kingsley Appiagyei as its first black student on placement from Spurgeon's College.[43]

Crofton Park was therefore already a multicultural church when I started attending in 2004, although it had a white majority of about 60 per cent, with the remaining 40 per cent black, mainly from the Caribbean. It was also an intergenerational church, with people of different ages and generations in attendance. The group that seemed to be lacking when I joined the church was young adults between the ages of 20 and 30. The ministers in 2004 were two white English ladies, Carol Bostridge and Sue Christie. Carol had become the minister in the year 2000, making her the first female minister in the

---

[43] After his placement at Crofton Park Baptist Church, Rev Kingsley Appiagyei went on to found Trinity Baptist Church in South Norwood. This is now one of the largest churches within the Baptist Union of Great Britain and has itself planted many churches, both here and abroad.

church's 92-year existence. [44] Carol and Sue empowered many women in the church, making Crofton Park a church which allowed women to participate fully and have leadership roles.

I experienced many culture shocks and theological differences at Crofton Park. This was obviously because I was new in the country, but I was also transitioning from a Nigerian Pentecostal church to an English Baptist church. One of the culture shocks I experienced was the worship style which, compared to the exuberance and expressive nature of my Pentecostal background, felt to me like being in a cemetery.

Another shock was the fact that I had to have a Criminal Records Bureau (CRB) check before I could attend youth meetings and gatherings. While in hindsight this was right, to me then it felt like suspicion and a rejection. This was compounded by the frustration of loneliness that many foreigners experience when they first arrive in a new country. As someone who had come from a culture where people talk to each other on public transport, even making friends in some cases, it was surprising to discover that this was not something that was encouraged in London; people were either reading their newspapers or not welcoming. Nevertheless, after I had been CRB checked and had given the church a letter of recommendation from my pastor in Nigeria, I started volunteering as a youth worker and later became a youth leader. I also became very involved in the wider life of the church, observing and learning the dynamics of a multicultural congregation.

I was doing youth work alongside other youth volunteers, and this was an exciting time for the youth work at Crofton Park as we started Soul United, a discussion group looking at different topics related to young people. I and another youth volunteer were also involved in facilitating Soul Brothers, a group committed to mentoring and coaching boys of secondary school age. Soul Sisters, a similar discussion group for girls, also existed.

Around the same time there was a home group for young adults running locally, called Synod. Synod was very special because it was a gathering of youth workers and leaders in the Brockley area. We

---

[44] Crofton Park Baptist Church was founded in 1908.

met to support one another, do Bible study, pray together and socialise. It was from this group that the decision to start a Youth Alpha course originated. The Youth Alpha was organised in 2005, and was a success as we were able to engage with a lot of young people from Brockley.

In 2006, another youth project started at Crofton Park. Two youth leaders from two different churches in Brockley met together in a cafe to discuss the possibility of a joint work between Crofton Park Baptist Church and Brockley Community Church. They came up with the idea of a youth club. The youth club became a great success as many young people came to have fun and engage with faith. As the club grew, we also had lots of young people on the waiting list. The youth club is still running today.

In 2005, while I was involved in youth work at Crofton Park and Brockley, I and a few other friends started an itinerant ministry by the name of Fire Starters. The purpose of this ministry was to impact young people for Jesus. We travelled to Bury St Edmunds, Chepstow and Colchester to speak in youth groups. Our speaking inspired many of the young people in these places, to the extent that some came to faith!

In 2004, I started working part-time at Tesco to support my post-graduate studies. My days and experience at Tesco were certainly an eye opener into the working-class life and culture in London. It was also valuable in terms of a multicultural context as workers were drawn from different backgrounds and parts of the world. There were Caribbean people, Africans, Eastern Europeans, Western Europeans, black British and white British. Lunchtime in the canteen at Tesco was always a time of separation as people tended to sit and eat with people of their own ethnicity. I managed to have friends across the cultures and ethnicities and was successful in that I was able to eat with any cultural grouping. When I started work at Tesco, I was doing night shifts, stocking the shelves with all sorts of consumer goods. This experience immediately opened my eyes to the consumer choices people have to make when buying anything, either for themselves or their animals (who have a whole aisle to themselves!).

The night shift also helped me to understand and appreciate the struggles that immigrants face in order to survive. Later, I started working at 6am which meant going to bed early and waking up very early to catch two buses to work. I combined this with doing a Master's degree in theology. Life was very busy and, to some extent, frustrating.

It was during this period of doing youth work at Crofton Park, studying for a Master's degree and working at Tesco, that I suddenly realised for the first time that I was a black man from Africa. While the people at Crofton Park were lovely and welcoming, it was frustrating for me when people tried to correct my English or ask me to speak louder because of my accent. College was good and helpful as the majority of us were from the global south, and therefore we had something in common. But my experience at Tesco was frustrating, especially when I was treated differently by some staff and customers.

In 2007, shortly after getting married to Lucy, a white English lady, [45] I became a student minister at Crofton Park serving alongside Carol. I stopped working at Tesco and enrolled for a Doctor of Theology degree as I had just finished my Master's. My role as a student minister involved teaching, discipleship and youth work. In 2008, after being recognised by the church, the London Baptist Association and the Baptist Union of Great Britain, I became an ordained full-time minister, making me the first black minister in the 100-year history of Crofton Park. This was very significant for the black people in the church, just as Carol's appointment had been for the women.

Carol and I worked as a team, sharing leadership responsibility and authority. This is significant because while Crofton Park was a culturally diverse church, most of the power was in the hands of the white majority. It must be mentioned that Carol had made significant efforts to change the structures so that under her leadership black people became part of the Diaconate. However, my accreditation as a Baptist minister and appointment as an ordained

---

[45] Being married to Lucy, a white English lady, has also enhanced my understanding of the English culture.

full-time minister meant that leadership was now fully shared. This put me in a position that enabled me to change structures and to encourage more participation of black people in the church. One suggestion I made was the introduction of African and African-Caribbean food at our elderly lunch club.[46] This led to the group having rice for the first time. One way I facilitated participation was encouraging the black people in the church to enrol in our leadership training programme. Many did, leading to greater participation and involvement of black people in the leadership and the life of the church.

After my ordination, some white people left the church; some for reasons unrelated to me, and others for reasons connected to me. More Africans and Caribbean people began to join the church, so the dynamics shifted to about 50 per cent white and 50 per cent black (with more Africans than before). My preaching and teaching had an African flavour to it, including using African customs and worldview in my sermon illustrations. This enabled people in the church to recognise and be aware that people are from different cultures and backgrounds; that is, not everyone is white English.

Being the first black minister did not come without its challenges. I remember someone in the church suggesting elocution lessons so that people could hear me properly. This was because a few people in the church complained that they could not understand me very well when I preached. In addition, some of the English people at the church expected me to pronounce English words with a perfect English accent, while no one could pronounce a single word of my language, Yoruba, with a Yoruba accent. Challenges will happen in any multicultural context, and this is why it is hard work for anyone involved. However, the challenges and frustrations at Crofton Park were nothing compared to the richness of the diversity that was present in terms of race, culture, ethnicity, gender, class and age. It was truly a glimpse of God's kingdom on earth.

---

[46] The lunch club, known as Welcome Inn, had a mixture of white British and African and Caribbean people attending. Most of their meals were traditional British food.

To God's glory, I can say that my ministry at Crofton Park was fruitful, particularly as many young adults were added to the church. One of the ways this happened was through a young adult's house group that I started called Ekklesia (the Greek word for 'church'). This group met fortnightly at our home for Bible study and discussion, and became a place for discipleship and friendship. Over the years the group grew, attracting other young adults from outside the church. The group is now very involved in the life of the church at Crofton Park through preaching, worship and even the leadership team.

After serving at Crofton for a total of seven years (four as a minister), Lucy and I sensed that it was time for us to move on. This was another painful decision but one that was necessary because God was calling us to move on. I started to pray and search for another Baptist church. I wanted to stay in Lewisham as I had built strategic connections with churches and ministers in the borough, and had become a borough dean with a good relationship with the local mayor. During this period I came into contact with one of the leaders of Catford Community Church, which was local to us, and was informed that the church had been searching for a leader for almost a year. Convinced that this was where God was calling me to next, I applied for the position and, after prayer and consultation, Catford Community Church appointed me as their pastor in September 2011.

This call was very significant, and I celebrate the fact that Catford Community Church was bold in choosing and calling me as their leader. It was a step of faith both for me and my wife and for the church, but God blessed us all as we stepped out of our comfort zones in obedience. Another factor that made my appointment significant was that it was an ecumenical partnership, as I was a Baptist minister now called to serve in an independent Charismatic church. The Baptist Union of Great Britain (BUGB) and the London Baptist Association (LBA) were both involved in the process and agreed to me being seconded to the church.

Catford Community Church started in 2002 as an Ichthus Christian Fellowship Church plant. It is now part of the Transform Network of churches which has a membership of six local churches.

It is a community church with a strong emphasis on family and friendship. The church also has a community centre on the high street where they run various projects and activities to build bridges into the community.

Reflections

In this chapter I have reminded us that Britain as a multicultural society in fact dates back to the foundations of the country. Over the years, people of different cultures have come to Britain, starting with the Celts in the first millennium BC. The post-war migration of Caribbean people was therefore a continuation of this process and not the start. Current public rhetoric is that multiculturalism has failed because immigrants have refused to integrate, therefore the UK government wants people to assimilate, disguising this as 'integration'. Racism and exclusion still exist in British society, therefore any discussion about foreigners integrating has to include tackling institutional and personal racism. The church is not exempt from racism, as the history of black majority churches reveals. However, while there is still the issue of prejudice and discrimination, there are some churches that are culturally diverse, serving as an alternative space of a radical community of God's people. This is God's kingdom on earth. My journey at Crofton Park Baptist Church is an example of a multiculturally diverse church having a leadership team that reflects the congregation.

I think my story is significant because I came as a missionary to plant an African church but intentionally left that project to join a British historic church. This church (Crofton Park Baptist Church) helped me to understand the dynamics of a multicultural context as well as understand the nuances of English culture. In addition, it gave me leverage and position to do mission beyond my ethnic boundaries. I have had to exercise patience and forgiveness as people have misunderstood and hurt me, but I thank God that the blessings of multicultural ministry have far outweighed the sacrifices.

My journey at Crofton Park was also important because I became the first black minister in its 100-year history. This enabled the church to be more aware and sensitive to people from other cultures and ethnic backgrounds, and also to empower black people within the church.

Chapter Six
Multi-ethnic or multicultural churches in Bristol?
Tayo Arikawe

There are not many people who choose to write their autobiography just for the sake of writing. For most people, an experience of life usually triggers their pen to do so. Though this is not an autobiography, it is an account of a significant part of my life and ministry, especially in the context of multicultural and cross-cultural mission in the United Kingdom. I welcome this opportunity to contribute to the ongoing discussion on reverse mission.

There are more than 50 books on my shelf that I have acquired in the last two years, and they have contributed immensely to my understanding of some of these issues. But I recognise that this is not an academic paper, so I do not intend to cite any of them. Simply, I want this contribution to be read as my story and theological reflections.

Personal and family profile

I am married to Calista Tayo-Arikawe and we have an energetic son, Mekus Tayo-Arikawe. I am Yoruba by tribe, from the south-western part of Nigeria, while Calista is Ibo from the eastern part of Nigeria. I trained originally as a geologist and mineral scientist (BSc) with some post-graduate training in exploration geophysics in Nigeria. In the UK I trained at Cornhill Training Centre in London, attaining a diploma in expository preaching. Currently, I am writing my MTh dissertation at the University of Chester via Wales Evangelical School of Theology. My thesis is on Paul's use of Scripture in 1 Corinthians 1–3.

Calista qualified as a pharmacist in Nigeria and has now requalified as a registered pharmacist in the UK. At the time of writing, our son is five and is in year one at school. He enjoys life in school and loves to visit his friends or come home with them after class. As a family, our first priority is to grow in grace and in the knowledge of Christ. We desire that our family and marriage should glorify God maximally. Therefore, we pursue together the ministry that God has given to us. I communicate God's word as a pastor-teacher while Calista gives me all the home and administrative support that I need.

Currently, I lead the multicultural forum of our church. The team comprises about 20 delegates from diverse cultural backgrounds. What I am getting the committee to do is to see the challenges in moving from being multi-ethnic to being a multicultural church.[47] To achieve this, we have to genuinely talk about the issues involved and then make recommendations to the church. I am hoping to help more churches in this way, and some have already approached me.

I also coordinate the work of Grace Evangelistic Ministries (GEM)[48] in Europe, which is part of GEM Worldwide based in Tennessee, USA. Our main focus is evangelism and mission. We are non-denominational and we partner with churches to do missions. Once a year we hold an annual conference with a view to bringing church leaders together. 2013 marks our third annual conference, and it is so amazing to see leaders from different theological, cultural and denominational backgrounds come together to share fellowship and ministry challenges together.

Salvation testimony

I was born and raised up in Ondo State in the south-west of Nigeria. My parents were devoted church members of the Methodist Church of Nigeria. Consequently, the Methodist Church became my church background. We went to church almost every Sunday morning and attended almost all church functions as my parents held responsible positions in the congregation. For my part, going to church was mainly for social interaction.

---

[47] Multi-ethnic meaning having people groups from different countries, but multicultural meaning the diverse cultures of these people being reflected in the mode of running the church.

[48] www.gemeurope.org (accessed July 2013).

In 1986, while I was at the University of Benin in Nigeria, God led me to an encounter with Christ through a campus programme I attended that was organised by the Christian Union (CU) entitled 'Encounter'. The visiting preacher for the evening was a man whom God had delivered from the occult to become a proclaimer of the gospel of Jesus, the same Jesus whom he had once hated!

When I arrived at the event, the preacher was testifying to God's deliverance of his life from the hold of Satan. One of the things that struck me most that night was his constant declaration that Jesus Christ is the Lord of all principalities and powers despite the prevalence of evil activities. As a young African boy, what I grew up to fear most was Satanic activities, especially in the form of witchcraft, which was very common in the small town where I grew up. So what led me to Christ wasn't so much where I would go if I died, as important as that is, but that Jesus is Lord of all things, including over those powers that I feared most. This was how the preacher articulated the redemptive message of the cross that evening. As soon as he made an altar call, I was the first person to stand up as I wanted to come under the Lordship of Jesus Christ. Following this confession, I was filled with the overflowing joy of salvation in my heart.

This reminds me that the gospel works in many ways in different cultural contexts. So for some cultures the gospel could be most relevant to the question of life after death; for others it could be the answer to the mystery of human pain and suffering, but all focused on the person and the work of the Lord Jesus Christ.

My spiritual journey

That night I was allocated a mentor who would take me through weekly Bible study. The surprising thing was that my mentor happened to have been a friend of mine in secondary school, so it was very easy for us to communicate. God used him tremendously to equip me for this lifetime journey. We read the Bible and prayed together for about three years before we both left that university. In the course of these three years it was obvious that my spiritual growth was very consistent, and as a result I was elected as associate pastor of our campus fellowship group. This was when I began to sense the call of God on my life. Later, I became involved with gospel work outside of the university as churches and pastors started asking me to help out with the teaching ministry in their churches. I was also involved in planting a couple of churches in the south-west of Nigeria.

The first Macedonian call

I had finally settled to pastor a youth fellowship group in 1997 when the door opened for me to leave Nigeria for the Gambia. The Gambia is one of the smallest countries in the world and is located on the beautiful west coast of Africa. It is popularly called the 'smiling coast of Africa'. Again, this opportunity for me was a case of God's providence. I knew I had a heart for mission but I didn't know how it would happen.

In 1996 a very good friend of mine had been invited to the Gambia to take up a teaching job. On arrival, he wrote to me asking me to respond to a 'Macedonian' call. I recall the words in his letter saying that the church in the Gambia was in infancy stage and he believed we could help out in our little way. This friend and I prayed about it for more than nine months before I became convinced that God was definitely asking me to step out into the Gambia.

The next hurdle was how to break this news to the youth fellowship for which I had already agreed to take up the pastorate. I remember the evening when it was announced that I would be leaving them; many burst into tears. Later I was prayed for and released to answer the next phase of God's call for my life.

I needed spiritual and financial support. Thank God for godly mothers! My mum didn't see any reason why I would not respond to God's call, so she decided to sell off her small business. With the proceeds from the sale of my mother's business, I bought the ticket for my flight and had a surplus of $30, which would have been about £16! It is this sum of money that I took as a reserve to the mission field.

In 1999, I was instrumental in starting a Bible class in Gambia that later grew to become an evangelical church, Grace Bible Ministries. This was the church that I pastored until I relocated to the United Kingdom in 2008.

The second Macedonian call

Our church in the Gambia hosted the pastor of a church in Cornwall, United Kingdom, for a week-long conference. It was through this pastor that I became connected with the church I now work for in Bristol. The pastor and this congregation had caught the vision of a multicultural church and so they wanted a pastor from another cultural context. I was invited to the UK to preach 'with a view',[49] and after a couple of months I was offered a pastoral job with the church in Bristol. This is how my family and I came to live in the United Kingdom. Again, we can see that it is only by God's providence that all of this happened.

Ministry in the UK context

When I arrived in the United Kingdom, the host church was more than 175 years old. They had come through a long journey of conservative evangelical Christianity, and regular attendance was about 300 to 400 people on a Sunday morning. There were only a handful of black people; the majority were white, middle class British. The church is situated on Stapleton Road in Bristol, a part of the city that is full of Asians, Africans and African-Caribbeans. Apart from the cultural diversity, Stapleton Road and the surrounding community is also rich with religious diversity, ranging from Islam and Hinduism to Sikhism and others.

---

[49] The phrase used to describe preaching in a church with a view to becoming their minister.

The senior pastor at this time had contributed immensely to making the church more Bible shaped and also more contemporary in terms of the general outlook of the church. I would describe him as very godly and very thoughtful about people and their needs. He had a passion to see the church become very multicultural, and this is the reason why I was brought into the leadership. The church is full of very warm and committed Christians, and they all welcomed me and my family very quickly. I realised that there was a great sense of corporate godliness in the church. I also observed that the church put a very high value on the faithful preaching of God's word, though from a Reformed Theology perspective.

At the same time that I started work at the church, I enrolled for part-time study at the Cornhill Training Centre in London for the next two years. This was for my personal ministry development, because up until this time I had been exposed mainly to doctrinal exposition that relied heavily on systematic theology. I hadn't realised that Cornhill was a place for beginners in ministry in the UK context. It appeared that all African and Asian pastors who came to Cornhill were somehow perceived as beginners in ministry, looking for knowledge from Western tutors! But this was not the case, as the majority of these pastors had already received some form of ministerial training back in their sending countries. For many, it was about understanding the context of ministry in the UK with a view to personal and well-rounded development in ministry. After all, Bible exposition is not a new thing in Africa – it is all that Scripture Union has been doing for decades all over Africa!

Challenges of ministry and mission in the United Kingdom

After a while, my welcome party and the honeymoon period at the church came to an end and the reality of foreign mission began to dawn on me. Some folks in the church started complaining that they couldn't understand my preaching for a number of reasons – my African accent, my use of 'big words', etc. Some said that I spoke too fast; for others it was about my style of preaching. Some didn't even bother to come to the service when I was the one preaching!

I saw the situation from their point of view and understood how genuine some of these comments were. Firstly, I preached with passion; maybe that was why I spoke really fast. Secondly, I hadn't learnt their conventional style of preaching – mostly with three points and three applications. I felt that they were used to a style that tried to find a direct connection to Jesus in every Bible text, even when He was not being referred to! This was very different from the way I preached. In addition, I was already a full-grown adult when I arrived in the United Kingdom, so no one should have expected my accent to change overnight. But I equally realised that many of our English brethren had a limited English and theological vocabulary (despite the fact that they spoke English and many had been in church for decades). Therefore some of them found it hard to understand what I was saying as they were not familiar with many of the theological words that I had used freely from the pulpit in Africa.

I struggled initially with the preaching style, which I later discovered is the standard of preaching in mainstream reformed churches in the UK – a story at the beginning of a sermon, with three points and three applications. But I must admit that it works well in UK churches. I also found it strange to see preachers reading their sermons from sheets of paper. An average African would think that such a sermon is boring and not from the heart, but I have come to realise that this is not the case. Some of these sermons are actually Spirit-filled, so what I struggled with was simply the fact that I wasn't accustomed to this style.

I had a challenge before me – how do I preach, or how do I adapt my preaching style? Do I continue with my usual doctrinal exposition or switch to a style of narrative-driven Bible exposition? At some point I decided that the most appropriate thing was to go by the style of the church. But in my attempt to do what they were doing, I really struggled in my preaching, and I am very sure many must have thought I was really an ignorant, rubbish preacher from Africa who had a lot to learn about preaching! Yes, I am happy to learn from my British brethren, and indeed have learnt so much from them. But one of my questions to this day is whether my British brethren know from a position of humility that they also can learn so much from Christians from other nations. They talk about learning from us, but this doesn't reflect in the posture of many, as far as I'm concerned.

I have come to realise that, unknown to many people, culture is a major influence on one's life and ministry, and there is no need to claim any superior position when it comes to style of preaching. Even our theology may have a cultural undertone which influences our preaching and our understanding of the Bible. However, whatever system of exegesis we may hold on to, it is at best an interpretive tool and can never replace the Bible itself. Common sense should teach us that it would have its own limitations and weaknesses, so we need the virtue of humility to continue to learn from one another, as long as Christ is the centre of our ministries. I believe this is what Apostle Paul teaches:

> And I pray that you ... may have power, together with all the Lord's holy people, to grasp how wide and long and high and deep is the love of Christ. (Ephesians 3:17-18)

Therefore, a mature understanding of Christ is obtained as we learn to listen to other saints of different theological and cultural backgrounds and hear what following Jesus means to them. By this I am talking not just about understanding the gospel, but also about understanding its full implications in Christ within the context of God's people.

Multicultural or multi-ethnic?

To the glory of God, I can say that more and more non-English people (Africans and Asians) have started attending our church. We are becoming increasingly multi-ethnic, but we are still far from being multicultural. By this I mean that we have people groups from different countries, but the diverse cultures of these people are not reflected in the mode of running the church. We have remained a white middle-class church in almost everything we do. Most of our sermons would appeal more to Westerners in the style of delivery, but all the same have been a huge blessing to all of us. We don't have a diversity of cultures in our eldership, but this may not necessarily be the fault of the church as they have to work within certain limits of people from other cultures who are available. As a church that sends out missionaries to Africa and Asia, we do not have any Africans or Asians on our missions committee. My point is that a church can be multi-ethnic but not necessarily multicultural, unless all of these issues and their implications have been thought through.

On the other hand, I have been to some black majority churches here in the UK and the above issues are exactly the same with them. Many churches that have been planted from Africa or Asia for the purpose of reaching out to the people of Britain are simply attracting black Africans or Asians. Church services, especially in the African-led churches, are done in the African way without any consideration of the possibility of participation of people from other cultures. It is a shame that many black majority churches in the UK don't see the divine prophetic agenda behind their ministries. Reverse mission has begun here in the UK, but many black-led churches are not intentional about this divine programme. God has brought us here to give the gospel back to a nation that is now full of pagans but once brought the gospel (though wrapped in Western culture) to us. There is so much spiritual decline in the UK that many churches are closing down at an alarming rate.

Apart from the non-white/white issues in the church, I have also observed that social and economic sub-cultures are big and real issues between the white middle-class folks and the white working-class Christians. If this is real among the white British, then it seems fairly clear that the black or Asian working-class folks don't have any hope of genuine fellowship with their white middle-class brethren. For example, the church holds an annual international Christmas party as an opportunity for us to share some good cultural fellowship together, but most of our middle-class brethren never attend this party. I believe this reflects a great problem with our understanding of the gospel and its implications for the genuine reconciliation of people from all nations, tribes and cultures.

In all of these challenges, our church is still one in a million in the UK and wants to keep her arms open to people from other nations. I do not know of any other church that has been intentional about being multi-ethnic. I know some brethren in our church, though only a handful, who are very intentional about embracing people from different cultures.

What I have said so far is all about sharing our struggles, and is not just negative criticism about our church.

Turning the table on mission: the way forward

Yes, there is a way forward; hence I would like to suggest some possible steps. First, the British church must accept that with respect to mission the table has already been turned by God Himself. The United Kingdom is a very needy mission field and desperately in need of spiritual help. Churches in the UK must adopt the posture of humility to receive help from their African and Asian brothers and sisters. God is now sending missionaries from other nations to this country. If our British brothers and sisters fail to orient to this reality, this would be a clear refusal to see God's handwriting clearly written on the wall. Therefore, the only respectable response from the British church is to offer a hand of fellowship out of a heart of love to missionaries that God is sending to this nation. I was very shocked when a well-known evangelical white British preacher said to me and some other African friends that he couldn't see any need for the presence of African pastors in the UK.

I am flabbergasted that many British Christians still want to raise money and fly off to distant lands for missions when their own 'Jerusalem' has become grossly heathen. It is good that missionaries are sent abroad, but we must retain some on home ground too. Sadly, some missionaries who go abroad behave like colonial masters – they go with a mindset of going to teach people but not to learn from them. This scenario happens because they mistake financial superiority for spiritual superiority.

This leads me to another point. The white majority and white British-led churches in the UK should be seeking ways to integrate and not just assimilate Christians from other nations into their churches. They should be speaking the language of spiritual friendship, or at least partnership, with missionaries or churches from other nations. For example, I know of a church where the British brothers and sisters still see the African, Asian and African-Caribbean Christians as just needy people who have come to church for help. While this is true in some cases, there is a deeper spiritual agenda to the presence of these people in UK churches.

The white majority churches should think seriously about integrating black and Asian leaders into their leadership forum. It is unfortunate that at times this is done just to prove to the outside world that a white majority Church is multi-ethnic but, in reality, power only revolves in the hands of the white leaders. This applies equally to black majority churches. The intention here must be real and genuine if it is to work.

On the other hand, African, Asian and African-Caribbean majority churches and missionaries must be intentional in their church planting to reach out to the people of the United Kingdom. This will involve extending a warm hand of fellowship to our British brothers and sisters and being willing to learn more about their context from them, with a view of doing missions together. We will not fulfil this prophetic agenda by gathering Asian, African and African-Caribbean people alone into our churches, except where demography warrants it.

In addition, the preaching of the 'health and wealth' gospel has plagued many churches. Godliness with contentment has been thrown out of the window. Unfortunately, this sort of teaching cannot expand the kingdom of God. I would encourage my fellow ministers to desist from this and develop a proper biblical theology of prosperity and healing and commit to teaching the truth to their flock.

We need lots of preparation for mission in Britain. Some of this will involve being able to speak clearly, not necessarily with a British accent, but linearly and slowly. I had to take some lessons. My experience in church is that British people listen in a linear direction and they get lost once the preacher digresses in the slightest direction. In the African context, it doesn't matter how much the preacher digresses; somehow we are able to understand what he wants to say to us, as long as he returns to the original point he was making. It means that our style doesn't work in the UK context.

When I visit some of the black majority churches, I see the same mistakes that British missionaries made when they came over to Africa. Somehow we still wrap the gospel in black culture and assume that our preaching is pure and undiluted. We need to realise how much our cultural backgrounds can affect our interpretation and application of the Bible. I am not saying that this is wrong in itself, but that we should be aware of the limitations it places on us, hence the need to be open to the input of others from other cultural backgrounds. In our church, for example, every sermon is rooted in reformed theology with little or no liberation motif.[50] Even when I am asked for a black African perspective on a Bible passage, what I think they really mean is that I should supply the application since they have supplied the interpretation. In other words, meaning lies in their hands while application is for the black preacher to determine since the black man's interpretation couldn't be trusted anyway.

On the other hand, the black churches are very strong in the liberation motif in interpreting texts, but have little or no idea about other types of theological reflections. Also, I still think that many black preachers have not learnt to articulate a Christ-centred liberation motif, so it leaves room for distortions in our preaching and consequent hindrances to genuine fellowship with our white British brethren who are coming from a different perspective. We

---

[50] Liberation here is used in the context of the Political Liberation Theologies, specifically the British Black Liberation Theology that has been developed in the UK since the 1990s through the work of scholars such as, but not limited to, Robert Beckford and Anthony Reddie. This theology, starting with the experiences of black people, is seeking to reinterpret Christian traditions and practices in the light of liberationist themes and concepts which arise out of black experiences. These liberationist themes and concepts are political freedom and equality with socio-economic justice for black and ethnic minority people who are usually oppressed and marginalised by white hegemony and structures.

assume that our shouting from the pulpit is a sign of spirituality and powerful preaching, but many times we have little or no content in those sermons.

On this cross-cultural mission field, we must not pretend that there are no challenges and problems. We must never be quick to quote passages of the Bible just to cover up these challenges. Rather we must engage seriously in honest and genuine dialogue. It is easy to say that we are one in Christ, but in practice some are more 'one' than others. We need to learn to celebrate the richness of our diversity. No wonder someone prayed that God should make us one but not all the same.

Another issue that requires revamping is our mission 'strategies'. What I have observed is that the church is at times so submerged in social works that the gospel proclamation and discipleship have been silenced in our evangelistic outreaches. I must say that the gospel has social implications, but social works without any gospel proclamation and discipleship will not be profitable for God's Kingdom. For example, giving hot cups of tea to homeless people on a cold winter's night is an excellent Christian service, but we must go beyond this to disciple them. This is the call of the Kingdom!

On the other hand, some churches deny the importance of social work that originates from sharing the love of God; they simply want to preach the gospel. This is also a wrong perspective. There are black evangelists shouting the Bible into the atmosphere in city centres without really connecting to anyone. This does not seem to work in the UK context. They could do better if they took time to ask our British brothers and sisters what works best in this context.

There is another dimension of ministry which amazes me – churches organise programmes and, because they do not want to risk being offensive to the invited guests, they intentionally leave gospel proclamation out of it. I have no doubt that this is a Western cultural problem. Have we become ashamed of the gospel? What we do not realise is that some of these invited guests know who the host is and what they represent, and some may be searching for truth and we fail to proclaim it to them. I am aware of some instances where churches have become good friends with non-Christian charities which unfortunately, in my opinion, will handicap them from being able to use this vantage position to affect lives to the maximum. Having said this, I don't want to underestimate the power of friendship evangelism if there is gospel intention behind it.

One thing I may have left out is the issue of the leader's authority, but as my former senior pastor pointed out when I asked him to read through this script, I should be sure that my criticisms are constructive. I have observed that in the UK the leader's authority is not taken seriously like it is in Africa. As my former pastor has rightly said, this may be due to postmodern influence or advanced democracy. But at the other extreme, our black majority churches are consumed with authority-oriented leaders to the point that people do not challenge the leadership's actions even when they are in the wrong. In fact, many of our pastors have taken advantage of people's gullibility to arrogate much power to their position, and there is much abuse of power in black majority churches today.

In conclusion, I want to remind us that the return of our Lord and Saviour Jesus Christ is more imminent than ever. So let us take His charge seriously to go and make disciples of all nations, in the context of the United Kingdom. The white majority churches must avoid the distraction of fighting for supremacy while the black majority churches must avoid the distraction of reacting to the supposed arrogance of the white majority churches. Instead, we need to hold hands and together march into this over-ripe mission field of the United Kingdom. And although there will be much tribulation (see Acts 14:22), we must keep on proclaiming that Jesus is Lord over the United Kingdom as we continue making disciples. May God help us all. Amen!

Reflections

Tayo's route to salvation and ministerial formation was through the Christian Union (CU) in Nigeria. Unknown to many Westerners, if you are involved in a CU either at college or university in Nigeria it is similar to being trained in a Bible college. This is because the ministerial formation at the CUs in Nigeria includes exposure to Bible study tools, prayer and fasting, city and rural missions and character building, all of which serve to build mature Christians. It is often said by church leaders in Nigeria that anyone who passes through the rigours and discipline that the CUs in Nigeria offer will be prepared for any kind of ministry. I can assert that this is true, as there are many examples that bear witness to that.

Tayo, like most of the others in this book, was already involved in mission work before relocating to the UK. His ministry in the Gambia was fruitful and successful before he was invited to the UK to serve in a church. The fact that Tayo was invited by his church in Bristol shows that there is need in the UK church for ministers from the global south, and that some British churches recognise this need. His involvement in church leadership in Bristol has highlighted what many black leaders face in a white majority congregation. One of the issues of such a journey is the shock and realisation that racial inequality still very much exists within church structures.

Tayo has also clearly pointed out that it is possible to have people from different nationalities in a church context, but this does not mean that it has become multicultural if power and structures still remain in the hands of white people. This is a concern that we have to ponder on. There is no point in having a black pastor to appear multicultural if we are not going to allow them to be themselves and bring in their own contribution. This is Tayo's sharpest critique, and one that is valid.

Finally, he also criticises black majority churches on their often authoritarian leadership style. The kind of leadership structures that are not accountable to the congregation and do not allow the church to criticise them have to be changed.

Chapter Seven
A call to the nations
Peter Oyugi

Early childhood

I was born on the shores of Lake Victoria in western Kenya in the small fishing town of Homa Bay. My parents worked as missionaries in the area, my mother having come from Finland as a missionary to Kenya and my father as a Kenyan. Life was often challenging for me as a child, I recall, considering we had to literally live by faith for our needs to be met. Financial support for ministry was pretty limited, as far as I could tell. Consequently I formed quite a clear picture in my mind that I didn't ever want to live as a missionary, since I had made my contribution in that area growing up as a missionary child.

The Christian Union movement

When I joined secondary school, I had to move away from home to study in a boarding school. The school was more than 450km from home, and this was my first experience of stepping out of my comfort zone.

It was while I was at boarding school that I made a firm commitment to follow Jesus as my Lord and Saviour. I became an active member of the Christian Union fellowship, an experience that would greatly shape my future, ministry and focus in life.

While doing my A levels, I started to feel a great desire to take the gospel across the nations of the world. I cannot recall how I came to this position. However, during our early morning prayer meetings at Alliance High School, I would often imagine visiting various nations to share with them the message of the Bible.

I continued with my studies and went to Moi University near the picturesque Rift Valley town of Eldoret, Kenya, to study electrical and communications engineering. I became an active member of the Christian Union there, too.

As a university student, I found myself fully immersed in service to God. Not only were we full-time students on campus but we were also full-time Christian workers. There were more than 600 members in the Christian Union, and we had meetings daily. I look back to that time and see it as extremely critical in developing me in my Christian faith. We had intensive evangelism, prayers and Bible studies on campus. It was a miracle how most of the Christian students passed their exams with good grades despite such busy lifestyles. We had no fear as students to proclaim Christ as Lord at every opportunity we had.

Answering God's call to service

While undertaking my final year at the university, I was praying for God to lead me to my next step. In my mind I was fixed on pursuing a successful engineering career. However, soon after doing my final exams, I was invited to work as an intern with the Fellowship of Christian Unions (FOCUS) in Kenya. This was the umbrella body for the student ministry on campus, and was affiliated to the International Fellowship of Evangelical Students (IFES). During the time I was a leader of the Christian Union, I had always struggled with having limited time to do God's work because of my studies. Now here I was being presented with an opportunity to serve the Christian Union movement with all my time, talents and treasure. I sensed with great fear that this was the path God was leading me into, but I stepped forward in faith.

At this stage, I could clearly see that my first decade of being a Christian had been greatly shaped by my being a member of the Christian Union. I had had numerous opportunities to practise my faith on campus and share the gospel with other students. Being a staff worker with FOCUS Kenya was simply another great opportunity to be involved in building God's kingdom.

My time with FOCUS Kenya opened the doors for further cross-cultural mission work. I was sent to the UK on a one-year missionary assignment in 1995, and went again from 2000 to 2003. Each time I was keen to return to Kenya to share my experiences and the lessons I had learnt.

Although in high school I had had a sense that I would serve in cross-cultural mission, for the time being that thought had left me. I was keen to strengthen the body of believers in Kenya through discipleship training. Any idea of a long-term mission abroad was not what I was looking for.

Becoming a missionary

It was during my time of ministry among students in the UK in 2003 that I first visited and spoke at Elmfield Church in Harrow, north-west London. Soon after that, I returned to Kenya and taught the Bible in the Christian Unions in universities and colleges. Although I was part of a local church in Kenya, the work among students took up so much of my time such that I wasn't able to be very active in the local church. I did, however, clearly understand that my service in the student world was very much part and parcel of building up the body of Christ.

In 2005, as I was preparing to take a sabbatical from student ministry after 11 and a half busy years, Elmfield Church invited me to serve them as their pastor. It took me and my family by surprise. Cecilia and I were married in 1998 and by this time we had two young children. Having already made two transcontinental moves in recent years, the thought of relocating again to the UK was daunting. After much prayer and reflection, however, we took this as God's call for us to be involved yet again in cross-cultural missionary service. So our move to the UK was in response to God's call to serve as cross-cultural missionaries.

Theological and missiological training

My previous work among students had exposed me to informal theological training through the many conferences I had been involved in, especially through the Ezra Bible Conference organised by FOCUS Kenya. I also did a theological studies correspondence course during that time. The Triennial missions' Conventions organised by FOCUS Kenya, called Commission, had also opened my eyes to seeing the need for missionaries in the world.

When I moved to serve at Elmfield Church, I started part-time studies in missions at a Master's level at Redcliffe College, Gloucester. I looked back to see how God's hand had always been over my life. Now I was serving God in perhaps the most strategic city in the world – London. There are people in London from every part of the world. I also began to see that God was bringing missionaries from the global south to reach the Western nations. Some came as career missionaries while other Christians came as professionals. It was evident that God's mission was from anywhere to everywhere.[51]

Coming from the global south to serve God in mission work was not an easy journey. In many ways, people did not see us as missionaries. There was a common perception that people coming to the West from the global south were economic migrants. Despite the UK being a much bigger economy than Kenya, deep within I realised that we had had to sacrifice so much to move north. We were often very lonely and isolated, and the sense of community even among Christians was lacking.

Elmfield Church is a church with Brethren roots. It was founded in 1933 and half of the congregation has been part of Elmfield for a long time. Around 20 or so years ago it made a shift to be more of an evangelical fellowship. One of the practices it still carries on from its Brethren heritage is that of having communion every Sunday.

---

[51] Bosch, D. J. (1991), *Transforming Mission: Paradigm Shifts in Theology of Mission*, Maryknoll: Orbis Books, pp.465-466.

Elmfield now has people from more diverse church traditions as well as people who are not originally British. It is a friendly church and has about 60 to 70 adults attending regularly and around 20 children. Those from churches of a Brethren background strongly subscribe to the priesthood of all believers, and this is very much in evidence in the work ethic of many in the way they undergo the practical aspects of church life.

One of the intentions that the leadership of Elmfield had when they invited me to come on board was to see the church reflect more of the cultural diversity of the local area, considering that it had previously been a majority white upper middle class congregation. My experience has shown that building a multicultural church takes a lot more effort and intentionality than building a homogeneous church. I have met people in the UK with a real desire to see this happen, especially in multicultural areas of UK cities, but there are certainly hurdles to jump. Culture is deeply rooted in us and shapes our values, attitudes and behaviour.[52] I have learnt many useful lessons through my experience of coming from Kenya to work in a predominantly white congregation.

Out of the comfort zone

The biggest change for me certainly was the one of having to live out my Christian faith in a different culture. This touches on several areas. For example, when going to church in Africa, I knew what to expect. The songs, the extemporaneous prayers, the sharing of testimonies of God's intervention in real-life situations, the preaching having a central place in the service and the enthusiasm of the church members all pointed to a sense of expectation that God would move in one's life. Church was a place to look forward to, a place to learn truths about God and also a place to catch up with others after the service.

---

[52] Adler, N. J. (1997), *International Dimensions of Organizational Behavior*, Third Edition, Cincinnati, Ohio: South Western College Publishing, pp.15-17.

A big difference for me in the UK was the sense with which people seemed to be conscious of time in church. Mind you, my church in Kenya had a set start and finish time, so I wasn't looking for everlasting services. Much of this difference is a question of how people view church. In my opinion, a major difference in this area is that church in Africa is a destination, a place of arrival, whereas in the UK it has felt more like a place of transition, a temporary stop for someone on a journey.

Closely linked to this is the role that music plays in a worship service. In Africa, singing is a deeper expression of emotion and devotion.

Despite efforts to seek to bridge the gap between the two different experiences of corporate worship, one has to accept that each local church has its own culture, and people tend to feel comfortable with a particular style. There is certainly nothing wrong with this, but it must be factored in when considering the challenges of crossing cultural barriers.

Every individual is different, and therefore some will be more flexible in adapting to new ways of doing things, and some are able to accept diversity without a problem. However, I soon realised that some of the Africans joining our services were not willing to adapt to this 'drier' way of doing church, and I don't blame them. Life in a different culture can be hard enough, and Christians look to church to be a place of solace where they can sense that they belong and feel accepted – a place where they feel safe.

Growing multicultural churches requires effort and much sacrifice. It requires vision to see what can come out of it. It involves a willingness to lay down one's life for others.

I would say that I have grown a lot during my time at Elmfield church as my weaknesses and shortcomings have been exposed by the sheer diversity that exists in terms of cultures, age, church traditions and worldviews. There are times when I have been frustrated by the speed at which change takes place. I have also often been misunderstood when giving people space to grow in certain areas of their lives.

Lessons learnt

If I were to be asked what is the biggest lesson I have learnt about being involved in cross-cultural missionary work, and especially when trying to build a multicultural congregation, without hesitation I would say it is the whole matter of helping people to be Christ's disciples. We as Christians need to understand that we are first and foremost called to be in Christ and only secondly to do things for Christ. It is only when we grasp this truth that we can show the commitment that is required to allow God to build His church at His pace. One could argue that this is a universal problem; however, I still believe it creates a more acute difficulty in a multicultural church environment.

My time at Elmfield has been a time of discovery of the beauty and richness of diversity. I have recognised that Christ has called people from every tribe, language and nation to be part of His kingdom. I have appreciated that unity is not because we are similar, but it happens despite our differences. This to me is what the gospel of Christ is about. I certainly have not yet got used to eating jacket potatoes, let alone Brussels sprouts, but I don't allow culinary differences to stand in the way of something bigger that God is doing!

Grasping the call to be followers of Christ helps us understand the importance of relationships. For relationships to be healthy in the church there has to be love, sacrifice, intentionality and a recognition and acceptance of differences. This is foundational in breaking new grounds of missionary movement from the global south to the north. As we see God moving more people from the global south to the north, we will need to equip them by way of training, mentorship and exposure. Much has been written about the experiences of Western missionaries going to the global south, but very little about the movement of missionaries in the opposite direction.

God's bigger plan in the movement of missionaries

Much of my training in cross-cultural mission work has happened on the job as I have dealt with all the challenges that have come my way. However, having learnt these lessons, I am keen that others do not have to go through the same struggles without adequate preparation. We must keep improving the mission experiences of those from the global south. The Apostles Peter and Paul both understood the importance of training, equipping and developing others in the faith, and so did Christ Himself. Mission doesn't have to be about 'them and us', but rather it is about all of us working together for Christ's greater glory. If we are to truly practise *Missio Dei*, we must be ready to accept that God's mission is from anywhere to everywhere.[53]

Missio Dei is a term with roots in Latin meaning 'God's mission' or 'the mission of God'. If mission is understood to originate from God, then human beings are only participants rather than initiators of it. The idea of *Missio Dei* gained ground at the Willingen Conference of the International Missionary Council (1952)[54] where mission was understood to flow out of the very nature of God. This thinking finds its foundation in the doctrine of the Trinity. Such an understanding of *Missio Dei* carries great significance for contemporary missionary activity. The implication is that all sections of God's family have a role to play in this mission; no single group of people has the monopoly of participating in God's mission.

When one looks back to the time when this understanding had not taken root in theological and missiological circles, there was a feeling that mission was to expose the east and the south to the privileges of the West. This often was interpreted to mean making people from the global south adopt a Western lifestyle and values in

---

[53] Bosch, D. J. (1991), *Transforming Mission: Paradigm Shifts in Theology of Mission*, Maryknoll: Orbis Books, pp.465-466.
[54] Goodall, N. (ed.) (1953), 'Missions Under the Cross', *Addresses Delivered at the Enlarged Meeting of the Committee of the International Missionary Council at Willingen, in Germany, 1952; with Statements Issued by the Meeting*. London: Edinburgh House Press.

the name of Christianity. However, *Missio Dei* helps one realise that because all human beings are equally a part of God's creation, no one group is superior. This equality was brought to light effectively by the reformation. Witte writes:

> Among you, '[t]here is neither Jew nor Greek, there is neither bond nor free, there is neither male nor female; for ye are all one in Christ Jesus' (Galatians 3:28; cf. Colossians 3:10–11; Ephesians 2:14–15). These and many other biblical passages, which Luther highlighted and glossed repeatedly, have long inspired a reflexive egalitarian impulse in Protestants. All are equal before God.[55]

This greatly influenced the acceptance that missionary activity was to flow from any place in the world to every place. Even sections of the church that are relatively poor socio-economically have a mandate and a privilege from God to participate in God's missionary activities. God's mission is advanced through the work of the Holy Spirit and is not dependent on one's status.

Global trends

As one observes the growth of Christianity in the world, one realises that the centre of Christianity has gradually moved south. Jenkins writes:

> Over the last century, however, the center of gravity in the Christian world has shifted inexorably southward, to Africa and Latin America.[56]

---

[55] Witte Jr., J. & Marty, M. E. (2002), *Law and Protestantism: The Legal Teachings of the Lutheran Reformation*, Cambridge: Cambridge University Press, p.301.

[56] Jenkins, P. (2007), *The Next Christendom: The Rise of Global Christianity*, New York, NY: Oxford University Press, p.1.

This is further affirmed by Johnson who states that there has been a dramatic shift of Christianity to the global south.[57] This is caused by the fact that more people in the Caribbean, Africa, South America and Asia are responding to the gospel message. With the increasing numbers of Christians responding to the gospel in the global south, and consequently to the call to be involved in missionary activity, we are seeing more and more Christians moving from the south to the north (also commonly referred to as the West) to take up leadership roles in Christian organisations and churches. [58] Carpenter affirms that southern and eastern Christianity is providing the global church with new leaders.[59] Some, of course, come as professionals to take up secular jobs.

It has been observed that the growing numbers of Christians from the global south indeed have a passionate enthusiasm for mission and evangelism that has mostly been carried out within the south so far.[60] There are 'promising signs of growth, as southern Christians begin evangelising the north'.[61] It is therefore a realistic expectation that these growing numbers of southern Christians will resource the need for gospel workers in the global north.[62]

---

[57] Johnson, T. (2007), World Christian Trends, Update 2007, *Lausanne World Pulse* [online], August 2007, Available from:
<http://www.lausanneworldpulse.com/766/08-2007?pg=1> (accessed 9 July 2012).

[58] Jenkins, P. (2007), *The Next Christendom: The Rise of Global Christianity*, New York, NY: Oxford University Press, pp.244-250.

[59] Carpenter, J. A. (2004), 'The Christian Scholar in an Age of Global Christianity', The Conference on Christianity and the Soul of the University, March 25-27, 2004, Baylor University, p.3.

[60] Jenkins, P., *The Next Christendom: The Rise of Global Christianity*, p.14.

[61] Ibid, p.17.

[62] Ibid, pp.244-8.

Partnership models

This calls for a willingness on the part of the church in the West to partner with those in the south. This may require a paradigm shift in historical thought patterns. Partnerships that have paternalistic attitudes or that create a dependency will not be helpful.

From the New Testament we learn that partnership should include the sharing of the following:

- Gifts (Ephesians 4:11-13; Romans 12:6-13) – the picture of the church being a body in which each member does its part to build the whole.

- Resources (2 Corinthians 8:4-12; 9:10) – here I am thinking of material resources in particular. It entails a mutual partnership where there is commitment by both sides to identify with the needs of the other even though the amounts given may vary from place to place. This demonstrates the bond of unity.

- Experiences (Romans 5:5-10; Philippians 3:10) – this demonstrates the ability to identify with each other. It will involve sharing not only in the hope that the gospel provides through Christ's death and resurrection, but also in the sufferings of Christ.

Necessary conditions

The pre-requisite for healthy mission partnerships is first that people from all nations involved must be willing both to give and to receive missionaries. Second, they must see themselves as part of the same body, and hence equal partners.

Empowering missionaries
However, we cannot ignore the following needs:

- **Training.** Harley has accurately captured the need and importance of training for those from the global south, whom he refs to as those from the Two-Thirds World.[63] If missionaries from the global south are better prepared, it will certainly make their missionary endeavours in the twenty-first century more sustainable and effective if we are to truly practise *Missio Dei*. We must always humbly remember that the gospel is a gospel of grace proclaimed by grace.

- **Affirmation.** This is done by allowing the missionaries coming to the West as either career missionaries or as professionals to be involved in church life and in shaping the mission of the church. It will also involve taking risks as we allow diversity in the way people express their faith in Christ as Saviour and Lord.

- **Opportunities.** Paul wrote, 'And how can anyone preach unless they are sent?' (Romans 10:15). Here he must have had in mind the need both for preachers and for opportunities to be available in order for God's mission to be facilitated. There are many people in the global south today who are responding to God's call and who are willing to cross cultural and national boundaries to proclaim the gospel of Christ. The churches in the West can, therefore, actively create opportunities for this to happen as it will bring blessing to His work.

Open doors

Now that God is already moving people from one part of the world to another, let us hope that opportunities for ministry will continue to open up. Efforts will have to be made to ensure that training is provided for the new missionaries coming from the global south and that they continue to be affirmed in the work they do. This does not mean that those coming from the West are no longer needed. Both are necessary. However, one must not fail to recognise this unique moment in history when there is a new missionary force arising from the global south that should be embraced with humility, gratitude and gladness. It will also be important that

---

[63] Harley, C. D. (1995), *Preparing to Serve: Training for Cross-Cultural Mission*, Pasadena, California: William Carey Library, pp v, vii, 8, 9, 123.

suitable mentors and pastoral care is provided for younger cross-cultural missionaries in order to enable them to give of their best.

Reflections

Peter Oyugi's story is an important one. First, his parents were missionaries – his mother was a missionary from Finland to Kenya. Although Peter admits that his parents being missionaries initially discouraged him from thinking of becoming one himself, this position later changed. I believe his parents being missionaries prepared him for the task of overseas mission.

Another important factor to note is that Peter is of mixed race, his father being Kenyan and his mother Finnish. This dual heritage and upbringing prepared Peter for understanding different cultures, and later became valuable as he worked in a multicultural context. His Christian Union ministerial formation was important in equipping him to work in a diverse cultural context such as London, as Christian Unions are inter-denominational and inter-tribal.

Like Tayo, Peter was invited by a church in the UK to be their pastor. This is important as it reflects that Britain needs more church leaders from the global south. He was the senior pastor or lead pastor of Elmfield Church, a multicultural church that reflects all nations. Peter's ministry in the UK was not restricted to the church as he serves in other capacities as a Christian Union representative working among students in this country.

Peter's plea that the West should partner with the missionary gifts that God is sending from the south should be taken seriously. In addition, his suggestion and insight that Christians from the global south need to engage in cross-cultural training is very important.

Peter is currently serving as a mobiliser for African Inland Mission (AIM) in the UK. AIM is an evangelical interdenominational missionary society involved in church planting, evangelism and training.

SECTION C

ASIA

The history of South Asian Concern (SAC)
Ram Gidoomal CBE

Sri Lankans in London
Harry Tennakoon

Chapter Eight
The history of South Asian Concern (SAC)
Ram Gidoomal CBE

The material from this chapter is adapted and used with permission from a book about South Asian Concern that is pending publication.

Forced migration

Whether it's a chosen path or a forced decision, immigration to a foreign land can have a profound effect on individuals and families. I'm speaking from experience here, as someone whose family experienced migration twice. For my family, the journey has been tough at times, but by the grace of God our story has had a happy ending thus far. But for other South Asians,[64] displacement can lead to broken hearts, broken families, isolation and deep, deep culture shock, and these individuals have very much been on my heart across the years that I have been working with South Asian Concern (SAC).

My family were double migrants, having moved country twice in one generation. The largest migration of South Asians in history occurred in the 1947 partitioning of the subcontinent into two nations – India and Pakistan – on the basis of religious differences. In just nine months at least 18 million people – Hindus, Sikhs and Muslims – were forced to flee their homes and became refugees, and at least a million were killed in communal violence. Our family was one of the many that was displaced during this time, moving from Sindh Province to East Africa.

---

[64] Southern Asia comprises the countries of Afghanistan, Bangladesh, Bhutan, India, Maldives, Nepal, Pakistan, and Sri Lanka.

Leaving home

Our second move came at the time of our expulsion from Kenya in 1967, when many Asian families were forced to leave East Africa by the then government, losing businesses and livelihoods that they had built up over decades. We had been more fortunate than many people in the years leading up to this expulsion from Africa. Having been established and successful business owners, with ventures in India and Africa, my family were able to create and develop businesses again soon after landing by ship in Mombasa, Kenya. We worked diligently over a 20-year period, led by my father and his younger brother, and life was prosperous for us.

So when we were forced to migrate for the second time and leave behind our home in Kenya, it was a real blow to our family, particularly my father's generation. Our assets and funds were frozen, and this made it difficult to withdraw money and take it out of the country. We lost much of our wealth in that way.

Pakistan hadn't wanted us because we were Hindus in a Muslim country. We had been rejected by India because we had chosen British citizenship rather than Indian nationality when independence beckoned. We were no longer welcome in Kenya because we were not African. Great Britain was our best option.

Arrival in Britain

I can still clearly recall my arrival in the UK, at the age of 16. Everything seemed so strange, I might as well have landed on Mars, such was the unfamiliarity all around me. I remember the unexpected nature of the move, the freezing cold weather, the sights and smells and the alien food – all so different from what I was used to.

Our life in Britain was centred on family and work. We developed a business of corner shops – convenience stores that were open for long hours. Fifteen of us slept in four bedrooms above the shop as we started from scratch again and faced an unfamiliar culture. On the one hand, we were in shock from leaving everything behind and having to start again. As a family we faced humiliation and disgrace, which was particularly hard for my older relatives who had worked so hard to establish thriving businesses in Kenya. But on the other hand, while the older generation was fed up, I was part of the younger generation who felt that it was time to rise up and take advantage of the new frontiers before us. So the younger group took charge, as the spirit of survival kicked in, with a new determination to rebuild our family name and business and restore what we had had before. Within six months, we had bought a second shop.

Community

Over time, we rebuilt in Britain and experienced the joys of close community, South Asian migrants supporting one another, with siblings, uncles and aunts all working together. Our community was willing to support us in various ways, and we had connections that stretched from the south of England up to Manchester who were willing to lend us money.

But while we had positive community spirit, there was also a pulling up of the drawbridge. As a family, we banded together and replicated the culture and community that we had enjoyed back home. We didn't really need the outside world when we had each other. The extended family met every Sunday – 50 or 60 of us! We set up our own social networks, and there was little incentive to integrate.[65] One of the key issues that South Asian migrants face is whether to integrate into their society or to stay separate. In integrating into the culture, something gets lost along the way, but if you do not, you can face a cultural dislocation that can lead to feelings of loneliness and isolation. Incidentally, this is something

---

[65] I talk in more detail about my experiences and observations in the book *Sari 'n' Chips*, which I wrote in 1993, published by South Asian Concern (SAC). It is about Asian culture meeting Western culture and is based on my own experience, though it also looks at issues more widely.

we are sensitive to at SAC, having experienced these cultural challenges first hand.

As for myself, while facing up to the cultural changes and challenges of Great Britain in the early 1970s, I was blessed with spiritual rebirth after hearing and responding to Jesus the Lord.

Coming to faith

As a young man living and working in the UK, I enjoyed reading a particular Scripture Gift Mission tract, not knowing it was from the Bible. I remember reading the words and enjoying them, and appropriating them for myself, meditating on them as I had done with my own (Indian) scriptures.

One day, I heard a talk by a Campus Crusade group in a pub, where they spoke about the same words that were in the tiny booklet in my pocket. I recall getting into an argument with them, and they agreed to see me in my room so that we could have a discussion. They left me with a New Testament, *Good News for Modern Man*. Having read it and carried out my own research about the historic truth of Jesus and biblical matters, I realised that this all had a lot of merit, and that I was being biased by downplaying Jesus, and showing enormous prejudice. You see, I was a physicist, and of course I felt that scientists had all the answers! But when I read the gospel, it challenged my mindset. I took Revelation 3:20 seriously – 'Here I am! I stand at the door and knock' – and I opened the door to faith by opening my windows, kneeling and praying to Jesus, asking Him to come into my life and be Lord of it. My journey began in humility and faith. It was October 1971.

Common ground

In terms of the changes I personally experienced after coming to faith, these were centred on believing, behaving and belonging. When it came to believing, I confronted what it meant to follow

Jesus as someone from a Hindu background, so I had to grapple with many theological translation issues.[66] To some extent, I loved finding words from the Vedas (Hindu scriptures) – from one theological dictionary, as it were, and trying to apply it to another, although I was careful not to violate or dilute the teachings of Jesus (which even many churches do!). I have found that, when grappling with two different worldviews, it has been helpful to focus on what unites them, rather than on the differences, and this has also helped me to communicate with my family about matters of faith.

So, for example, the Vedas allude to the sacrifice of Christ and declare sacrifice as the only way for salvation. *Dharmani prathamani* means that sacrifice is the most important of all our duties. In other places, the Vedas write: *Yagyo vay bhuvanasya nabhih* – sacrifice is the base of the world – and *Ritasya nah pathinay ati vishvani durita* – get saved through sacrifice. The Shatapatha Brahmana says: *Prajapathi yagyah* – God Himself is sacrifice.

Furthermore, Rig-Veda includes the following facts, among others, regarding one of the sacrificial animals: that it should be a lamb without blemish; around his head a *balasu* bush should be placed; it should be on the altar of sacrifice; no bones should be broken; and after it is sacrificed, it should come back to life again. There are so many echoes of Christ's journey to the cross and of His sacrifice for our salvation. I have also looked at equivalent concepts such as duty (*dharma*); creation, sin and sowing and reaping in the context of eternal life (*karma*); and the red thread in our Hindu traditions, which can be considered the blood of Christ, covering the believer.

My approach has been to try and understand one within the other, all the time trying to shift the lens of that camera and look for a point of convergence. Naturally, I have faced criticism for this, but it's worth it for the sake of understanding the teachings of the Bible in terms that make sense to people with my background.

---

[66] I have explored these in depth in my book *Karma 'n' Chips* (1994) published by Wimbledon Publishing Company Ltd, but to summarise, I see many echoes and similarities between the teachings of Jesus and the teachings of the Indian scriptures.

Believing, behaving and belonging

On a more practical level, I was still fortunate to belong to my community, as well as the community of people who follow Jesus the Lord. As for my family, they observed me very closely. As a new follower of Jesus, I still ran my business in a certain way but increasingly found that any unethical ways were challenged as I read the Sermon on the Mount and the rest of the Bible. My family also held me to account, which encouraged me to behave with integrity. This included not overcharging, making every effort to find the right price and being honourable in my business dealings: simple behavioural changes. To my family, I found that I was representing all Christians, whether they were Catholics or Protestants.

My experience of Jesus also brought me peace of mind, which I had previously lacked. I was deeply troubled before, but afterwards I slept like a log. My Hindu practice of reading, reciting and meditating on words of scripture also enabled me to effectively meditate on the book of Psalms, to reread them like mantras, and this was a very useful discipline that translated across the two belief systems and shows how, as people of faith, we can learn from each other.

Lost in translation

I feel that it is very easy for South Asian Christians to stay separate from mainline churches in this country. There are so many factors that make it difficult to integrate with the body of Christ.

One of the issues I faced when I became a follower of Jesus was which church I should go to. I had no idea whether I had become a Catholic or a Protestant, so which church should I choose? The nearest church to my halls of residence was the Church of Jesus Christ of the Latter Day Saints – a Mormon congregation. However, I did not know whether I could just go in or whether I needed an invitation, and there was no one I knew who could take me. So I decided to continue reading the Bible by myself.

Eventually, an Asian student, Ranil Pereira, saw me eating meat and asked me about it, having assumed I was a vegetarian Hindu. I explained that I was following the Bible which says if you give thanks, Jesus says pretty much any food is okay. Ranil encouraged me to join the Christian Union and I became a regular member. Later, two students on my physics course invited me to an evening service at St Paul's Onslow Square. The vicar at the time was Raymond Turvey, and I loved the songs we sang and the messages.

Culture shift

At first, attending St Paul's was difficult because I wanted to take my shoes off and there was no rack for them! The music sounded like a funeral song to me, as I was used to celebrating lively Asian festivals, such as the Hindu Diwali, and Khushiali with the Ismaili Muslims. Many of my English friends couldn't understand what I was going through, and a few suggested I change my name, or leave my family. But for the most part, they were afraid to ask questions because of political correctness. Fear and respect made them hold back. This is a very real, very practical point for many British people: the tendency is not to ask questions because religion is thought of as a private matter.

On the contrary, there is actually no harm in asking people questions about whether they are making friends and how they are finding their way around the whole complicated body of organisations that call themselves by the name of Jesus. Sometimes there is shyness, a lack of boldness, or perhaps a fear of anything that is unfamiliar. In addition, while there is a trend in society for all other religions to be recognised, it can be a different story for the churches. Consequently, Western Christians are generally shy rather than bold. This is quite a challenge and can be misinterpreted by some of us as being non-welcoming, or even racist. But that is not the intention of most Western churchgoers.

When I realised that I could not really take my family to church, we organised a meeting in my brother's flat in Southall, as he had also become a follower of Jesus. We invited family members, sang songs in Hindi, and studied the book of Ruth, also in Hindi. These were great times of singing and prayer, and we all loved them. Through that, several family members had spiritual experiences as they also became followers of Christ.

Looking back

In the 40 years that I have been a follower of Christ in Britain, many things have changed, and many other things have stayed the same. There are now many more South Asian followers of Jesus in the nation, but the attitude of traditional churches has not changed significantly with regard to us – there is still a 'them and us' mentality. However, we stand at a significant point in history, where the number of South Asian followers of Jesus is such that together we can make a difference. Technology exists to link people together, and there are new and exciting forums where South Asian followers of Jesus can be heard and can build friendships, both with each other and with the mainstream churches.

As I discovered when I became a follower of Jesus, there is a lot of common ground with Hindu thought and practice, despite the differences. People from different cultural backgrounds who follow Jesus the Lord find themselves infinitely closer to each other in Him. So South Asian followers of Jesus and the mainstream churches should be able to work together to find their common ground, embrace each other, and experience a deeper level of unity.

History of South Asian Concern (SAC)

All great kingdom initiatives start with God, and South Asian Concern (SAC) is no different. God is the one who motivates people to engage in exciting, culture-changing adventures – ones that start small but go on to advance the gospel powerfully as they touch the lives of countless people for the glory of God.

The seeds of SAC were sown in the hearts of a handful of individuals. Each one had their own unique skills and specialities, and a part to play in birthing, establishing and expanding the work to which God had drawn them. Their individual stories are noteworthy, and are interesting because they illustrate how God reveals Himself to diverse people today through His love and grace, equips them fully for His work with different skills and experiences, and calls them both individually and corporately to build His kingdom. This has been the story of the gospel from the start, and the team at SAC will gladly tell you that they feel honoured to be caught up in the grand narrative that spans the centuries.

Seeing the need

Dr Raju Abraham, Robin Thomson, Professor Prabhu Guptara and I were compelled, both individually and together as a group, despite our differences, to serve the needs of South Asians, particularly followers of Jesus, and to see the gospel flourish in the UK and abroad. Over time, more people joined us.

My wife, Sunita, and I met Raju and Catherine in summer 1987, and that August we invited them and Prabhu, who is a Hindu follower of Jesus, to our home in Sutton. During our conversations, Raju spoke about the political, social, economic and spiritual needs of the Indian subcontinent, and gave his observations as a medical scientific professional. Prabhu gave his thoughts on India, and on his work in north India from his standpoint as an academic and a business professional.

Later, Prabhu became the executive director for organisational development at Wolfsberg, a subsidiary of UBS, one of the largest banks in the world. He was involved in supporting the work of SAC from the beginning, and has provided significant amounts of prayer, finance and business consultancy, mainly from a distance, as he lives in Switzerland and works internationally as a business executive and lecturer. I also had an interest in India from a business perspective, as my family had an office in Bombay, trading tea from their estates in Coimbatore.

I candidly admit it was fascinating to hear Raju and Prabhu, but I still didn't see my role in it all. I had lost my connection with South Asia, having been brought up in East Africa and moved to Britain. Survival was my major concern: when I came to Christ, I only saw my duty and responsibility to share my spiritual experience with my family and community – not other South Asians, let alone British people. I didn't know enough about the geography of the Indian subcontinent and its sheer diversity, nor did I fully appreciate my own roots and history. However, my interest in these areas started as a result of my spiritual experiences, and it was at that lunch that the seeds were sown. I then continued the conversation with Raju, meeting at his house or mine, or in my office in Belgravia.

Slums and ghettos

In April 1988, I had a life-transforming trip to India, where I saw the poverty and desolation of Bombay's slums first hand (now Mumbai). I was on a business trip to buy prawns from the Indian subcontinent for sale in the European market, and on the last day of my trip, at Raju's suggestion, I met up with his brother Viju Abraham. Viju was part of the International Fellowship of Evangelical Students (IFES) in India, and had previously been involved in planting evangelical student fellowships in Bangladesh, Nepal and Sri Lanka. He was now serving people who lived in the slums and ghettos of Bombay.

Thinking that Raju had sent me to be shown around the slums, Viju dutifully led me, along with a group of Christian pastors from different denominations, through Bombay's shanty town. I was not prepared for what I was about to experience. Viju introduced me to the rag pickers, the prostitutes' children, and the poorest of the poor. I was absolutely devastated by the appalling sights I saw. I couldn't believe it. The pastors also told me about the so-called 'slumlords' – imagine having to pay rent to live in a slum! I saw child prostitutes of about five years old, one of whom reminded me of my own son. He didn't even have a pavement on which to sleep.

During the plane journey back, in my first-class cabin, I broke down. I just couldn't take the caviar and champagne that was being offered. How could I be a follower of Jesus and live in such conspicuous luxury, doing nothing about what I had seen? When I came back I was completely downcast and thought, 'What can I do with what I have seen?' Every day God was weighing on my heart. I thought to myself, this must be what God's calling feels like – the overwhelming need to respond to the sheer horror and devastation I had experienced there.

Life change

My wife Sunita comments:, 'On Ram's return from India, we spent a lot of time talking and praying about what he had experienced, and the future.' My family returned to London from Scotland, where we had been living for the past year, and I then handed in my notice at the Inlaks Group, an international conglomerate of which I was UK Group Chief Executive. In July 1988 I therefore gave up what I would describe as my 'plush, well-paid job'. It was a step of faith, but I had been strongly led by God to do it in order to concentrate more on philanthropic ventures and to serve God by harnessing my business acumen.

I continued working with the company in central London, but reduced my days. Around this time I met Steve Chalke at a meeting at my offices facilitated by Raju. Raju had previously encouraged Steve to visit the same slums, which he had done in February of that same year. Steve had also been deeply moved by the experience. Raju explains, 'Steve's parents were from India, and he had received from his parents a very nostalgic idea of the nation and thought of it as a fantastic place. He got in touch with my brother Viju who showed Steve around the slums, and he was appalled by the India that he saw. He came back to England and rang me up, saying he had met my brother and had an idea of an initiative in the UK that could raise funds for Viju's ministry in Bombay.'

The fruit of that meeting between Steve and me was the highly successful Christmas Cracker initiative, which proved to be foundational for SAC. Let me digress a little by telling you the story of the Christmas Cracker, before going back to the fourth person involved in the foundational stages of SAC.

1989 – Christmas Cracker

In 1989, Christmas Cracker exploded onto the UK's fundraising scene. The innovative Christmas Cracker scheme enabled youth groups to open temporary restaurants with an invitation for people to graciously 'eat less and pay more' for a meal. The idea was to offer 'First World prices for Third World grub', with all the proceeds going to famine relief in the developing world.

This initiative, begun by Raju and me, along with Steve Chalke and others, embodied many of the values that SAC would go on to embrace. These included the ability to mobilise and unite followers of Jesus for the sake of raising significant funds to serve the poor, and to support initiatives across faith groups. Although it was a separate initiative, and not strictly an SAC project, SAC was very active in organising and directing the Christmas Cracker charity.

Good friendships
It cannot be underestimated how important good friendships and working relationships are in successfully establishing and continuing community work. Steve and I hit it off from day one, both having an entrepreneurial, go-getter spirit. My strength was as a businessman, and Steve's was as a youth worker with a vision and a sense of mission.

Raju and I knew that Steve had been instrumental in the creation of Beggars' Banquet, a temporary restaurant in Tonbridge which raised money for the poor. I envisaged branding and franchising this restaurant idea and running it across the country. If hamburger chains could be nationwide, why not charity restaurants, set up in temporarily vacant high street shops, borrowed from their owners?

Raju brought in his keen focus and links with his brother Viju's critical work with the poorest of the poor in Bombay's shanty towns.

Raju, Steve and I met up at my Belgravia offices to develop the idea. We agreed that Christmas Cracker would happen in the four-week run-up to Christmas, hence its name. Having significant experience in business, I was able to drive and develop the business case for Christmas Cracker. With any new business idea I always ask ten questions, and this was no different. These questions are: What do you want to do? Why? Why this? Why now? With what? By whom? By when? How much? What are the consequences of doing it? What are the consequences of not doing it?

Getting the brand right was essential, but the team wasn't comfortable with retaining the name Beggars' Banquet because of its negative connotations. So they brainstormed a different name and came up with Christmas Cracker, an upbeat phrase that has overtones of festivity and gift-wrapped presents while including 'Christ', the reason for the season and the purpose of the initiative – to serve the Lord through philanthropic endeavours.

Next came the phrase 'eat less, pay more', along with many other wonderful marketing slogans, and so it was time to brand and advertise the initiative, as well as setting up the network of restaurants – which was no mean feat.

Outsourcing

Fortunately, the Christmas Cracker team was diverse, with many different skills and connections. I suggested that it would be sensible to keep the costs for Christmas Cracker as low as possible by outsourcing all operational processes. For starters, this meant not having a separate office or assets for the venture, but instead favouring service level agreements with different organisations.

From SAC's perspective, this meant offering business and administration services, including managing the documentation required by the Charity Commission, keeping the accounts, raising money to keep the project afloat, and reporting back to the various constituents. Key personnel, including myself and my wife Sunita, Robin and his wife Shoko, and Raju and Catherine all offered their expertise as unpaid volunteers.

Meanwhile, Christmas Cracker outsourced other parts of its operations. For example, Raju had a very good friend, an accomplished designer called Paul Clowney, who was part of the same group of followers of Jesus to which Raju belonged. Paul had a design and branding company and was instructed to develop the branding and graphics for Christmas Cracker. He came up with an innovative neo-Zulu design, as well as many of the memorable catchphrases such as 'Bite for right'.

Securing the funds

On Monday 12th December 1988 (which was, incidentally, the day of the Clapham Junction train disaster), the Christmas Cracker team convened a meeting of different denominations and organisations at Bloomsbury Baptist Church, London. At this meeting, two agencies agreed to provide the seed funding for Christmas Cracker, with a £5,000 interest-free loan from Interserve and a £5,000 grant from Tearfund. At the time, Raju was part of the Interserve council, representing African, Caribbean and Asian Christians, and was also on the reference board of Tearfund. I was able to raise the bulk of the finance, a chunky £60,000, from my family contacts. This enabled Christmas Cracker to go ahead and register as a charity and begin operations.

In its first year, 1989, Christmas Cracker ran 100 restaurants and mobilised more than 20,000 young people with Steve's valuable help, raising £400,000 to help India's poor. This also enabled it to pay back its funders quickly, giving them an additional £100,000 each for their charitable projects. 'They were absolutely stunned by this new approach to raising funds,' says Raju. But this was just the beginning, and the project was unbelievably blessed by God. Over a seven-year period, and through various initiatives, Christmas Cracker raised more than £5 million for various charities.

Working together

The creative use of business skills and links makes things happen. It gives me all the excitement of deal-making, not for making money for myself now, but for getting others excited, getting them to go beyond themselves – which is, after all, the reason that Jesus came to earth. The success of Christmas Cracker's first year helped it to secure further investment for the following year's programme. This was funded exclusively by a £50,000, interest-free loan from Tearfund.

Steve's extensive experience and connections in the sphere of youth work were vital in recruiting the youth groups and thereby securing the all-important staff for the restaurants. These young volunteers were required to attend a one-week course which gave them basic business skills such as accounting, and included a study of what the Bible teaches regarding poverty and mission. The great thing about this training was that it made people aware of the world's needs and enabled thousands of Christmas Cracker teenagers, aged between 16 and 18, to become catalysts for change.

The training course was designed and delivered by Raju and another key supporter, Lieutenant Colonel Brian Phillips MBE, who was associated with a publishing house called Elm House. The organisation produced magazines that included the titles *21CC (21st Century Christian)* and *Youthwork*, targeted at youth workers. The team was able to utilise these to publicise the Christmas Cracker project. *21CC's* editor, Hilary Armstrong, became an important member of the Christmas Cracker team.

The desire of our hearts was not just fundraising but also to excite young people, to make them aware of the issues that are faced by those in the not-so-well-off parts of the world, and to help them to do something about it. The feedback we received from participating youth groups was that this was the best thing they'd ever done. They gained credibility and increased their profile in the community. It was a different kind of giving – young people's time and energy.

The renowned cultural analyst and journalist, Jenny Taylor, who was editor and press officer at Interserve between 1988 and 1994, was seconded as Christmas Cracker's national launch press officer. Her work with Christmas Cracker won nationwide media coverage for a new concept in fundraising, including airtime on BBC Radio 4's *Today* programme. Jenny also organised and ran the launch event, 'The World's Biggest Christmas Cracker', on London's South Bank, which made it into the Guinness World Records.

As the project unfolded, *21CC* magazine was tasked with putting out regular features about the initiative and marketing it to its readership. Steve Chalke's youth charity, Oasis, was responsible for recruiting youth groups to operate the restaurants. Raju observes, 'We had a very creative thinker in Steve Chalke, who was able to mobilise 20,000 young people. Then there was Ram who had the lateral thinking and financial stability and control to steer the venture. We also had Hilary, who gave editorial input from *21CC*; and Paul on the design side. Paul devoted many creative hours to Christmas Cracker, and had many strange and wonderful ideas. The modern graphics and design that he came up with were fantastic, and really excited young people.'

Prabhu adds, 'Ram was full of imagination and energy, and came in like a breath of fresh air. He brought a mix of business skills into the picture at a time when no other person was doing so, and was bumping into the right kind of people. It was not something he alone could have organised! No one else was doing franchising, or training young people and raising money for charity on such a systematic and large scale. It immediately attracted attention because it was a "global first", a pioneering effort in the whole of the NGO sector.'

Channelling the resources

Each year, the charity's focus changed, with Christmas Cracker setting up an independent group to determine who would benefit from the significant funds that were being raised. The trust now comprised Raju, Steve, Lt Col Brian Phillips, Graham Mungeam and myself. As a group of trustees, we were required to define where the resources went, and decided from the beginning that they would go to organisations consisting of committed followers of Jesus carrying out social projects. In reality, Christmas Cracker was not just about money; it was about generating interest to engage a new generation in the 'Two-Thirds World'.

The first year it helped to support South Asia and the slums in Bombay, which had weighed so heavily on the hearts of Steve, Raju, myself and others. The money that was raised from the restaurants was also used to facilitate projects across India, including an initiative to drill wells and provide much-needed water for communities. Other projects were Ashirvad – (Hindi for 'blessing') which was designed to support disabled children and their families; and Nambikkai (Tamil for 'hope'), working with deaf people. In the second year, Christmas Cracker supported work in Uganda that centred on Aids, as one in three were dying from the disease, with funds also supporting initiatives in Africa more broadly, and indeed across the globe.

Radio Cracker

However, in its third year, the vehicle through which Christmas Cracker raised its money was community radio stations rather than Crackerterias. This was due to some new developments over health and safety regulations, which meant that running restaurants in empty high street stores was more problematic than in previous years! The team helped its volunteers to set up almost 100 community radio stations under the Radio Cracker brand, requesting listeners to send donations to play Christmas requests and send messages to friends and family. Pirate radio stations had been made illegal, which meant that individuals could buy the newly released FM bandwidths and transmitters, and the charity had registered with the government to do this.

After the restaurants and radio stations came newspapers. 'After the first year, we had to think up new ideas every year, but the point was that we were creating an atmosphere for young people to go into areas of service,' says Raju. In the third year, the charity channelled funds towards the Brazilian slums, working alongside Tearfund and Compassion. Christmas Cracker was involved in shooting a video to raise awareness of the *favelas*, the Portuguese word for slums. Then, in year four, 1992, Steve went undercover in Thailand's Red Light District to investigate and raise awareness of paedophiles and sex-trade criminals. The fifth year of Christmas Cracker had a focus on fair trade.[67]

---

[67] In 2012 I took on the role of Chairman of Traidcraft: Traidcraft is an organisation that fights poverty through trade and helps people in developing countries to transform their lives.

Over the seven years that Christmas Cracker ran, it raised more than £5 million for various charities and urgent needs. It also harnessed more than 50,000 volunteers, many of whom became interested in the world's needs because of the initiative, and as such the project was a great success both from its own perspective and for the SAC, which shared its objectives and vision.

One of my objectives in setting up Christmas Cracker was to demonstrate to mainstream charities working with young people that there are innovative ways of attracting teenagers to respond to the needs of those who are less well off than themselves. If these mainstream charities could be challenged to rethink their approaches to targeting and mobilising teenagers, then, given their significantly larger budgets and resources, they would be far more effective in raising even more funds and mobilising an even larger number of teenagers to respond to emerging world needs. The trustees observed a significant shift in the way that the larger charities were now approaching teenagers and decided after seven years that one of their key objectives was fulfilled, and therefore decided to wind down the charity.

South Asian Concern

Going back to the history of South Asian Concern, the fourth person who had a keen interest in work among Asians, particularly business people, was Prabhu, the corporate business management expert mentioned earlier. Prabhu knew Raju and also met me when he was working as a consultant, as he flew frequently to Geneva where I lived with my family before we moved back to the UK. Prabhu recalls, 'When Ram had moved from Geneva to England, and following his trip to India, he decided to leave the company he was working for. Ram was trying to decide whether or not to go somewhere to study the Bible full-time.'

Prabhu encouraged me to persevere in business, identifying four factors that made me unique in my work for the Lord. First, I am a Sindhi, with origins in Sindh Province, an area that straddles India and Pakistan and whose people are known for being pioneering, industrious and savvy in business. Second, I was a successful businessman, with God-given skills in this area. Third, I had personal as well as family and business links with Asians. And fourth, I could help non-Asians to understand India and the needs there. Everything was pointing towards the establishment of an organisation with a business edge that could serve the Indian subcontinent through fundraising, and South Asians in the UK through building friendships and partnerships. The vision and purpose for SAC were starting to become apparent.

SAC was formed after several months of regular meetings between Raju and me. We were later joined by Robin, who was working part-time with SAC and also with St John's Nottingham, based in Raju and Catherine's dining room. Prabhu was often part of those meetings. Raju, Robin, Prabhu and I continued to meet regularly to pray and progress this vision of South Asian Concern. Before long, others joined us. These included management consultant and businessman Deepak Mahtani, who moved to the UK from Geneva, Switzerland. Suneel Shivdasani was also integrally involved. He was a lecturer and IT professional who had spent three years in the shipping industry, two years as a financial consultant and eight years in the public sector in computing: programming, systems analysis and other areas.

Chatru and Jyoti Manglani were key members of the team and its daily operations for the five years that they were based in the UK, from 1992 to 1997. Chatru, a chartered accountant, served as treasurer for SAC, as well as the associated ventures Christmas Cracker, South Asian Development Partnership (SADP) and Winning Communications. Paul East became involved with SAC from 1993, bringing his significant management experience in the NHS, followed by 20 years in South Asia and the Middle East working in project management, strategic planning, personnel development and welfare.

Summary[68]

Charitable giving has always been a part of my life, which can be credited to strong religious influences. I was raised in both the Sikh and Hindu faiths and attended a Muslim school as a child in Kenya. At 16, I came to Britain as a refugee, and later became a follower of Jesus the Lord. All these strands were important motivators for my giving. Yet my visit to a slum in Bombay (Mumbai) shocked me into doing more. The experience made me realise not only how fortunate I was, but also how much of an impact I could have on others. Seeing this deprivation first hand put my own financial position into context. I realised that I was financially secure and privileged. I asked myself, 'Why am I working for this money? What good is it for?'

The Christmas Cracker initiative enabled me to use my business and entrepreneurial experience and also to motivate young people to be aware of global issues and get involved. Although I had initially intended to run the project for only one year, the enthusiasm of the volunteers encouraged me to continue. It was a very rewarding experience. We were changing lives while motivating young people to get involved. Many of the youth went on to careers in journalism, while others went abroad to work in relief efforts.

Believing that time and energy can be more important and meaningful than money, and inspired by the success of Christmas Cracker, I took early retirement at the age of 40 to focus on charitable activities. Today I devote my time to a number of charities in the UK, including Traidcraft, the Lausanne Movement, London Sustainability Exchange, The Employability Forum (helping refugees and asylum seekers find work), Citylife (helping disadvantaged individuals across the country find jobs and housing), and South Asian Development Partnership (a charity I founded in 1991 to facilitate and catalyse entrepreneurial initiatives in the UK and South Asia), to name only a few. I have also written a

---

[68] Adapted from *A Guide to Giving*, 2nd edition, Philanthropy UK, 2005.

number of books about ethnic minorities in Britain, and am a regular speaker and media commentator.

In my work I try to never lose sight of what is driving me. It is easy to forget or confuse why you wanted to give your time or money in the first place. I won't let myself forget the people in that slum in Bombay. Yet I believe the most important lesson I have learned from all these experiences as an engaged philanthropist is this: don't let what you cannot do stop you from doing what you can do.

Reflections

Ram Gidoomal's journey is fascinating on a number of points. His story exemplifies the migratory pattern of many people in diaspora. His family went through two forced migrations before they eventually settled in the UK. This sort of migratory pattern easily dislocates and disconnects families and communities, and Ram's family, though better off, were not immune from this isolation. His story of growing up and living in Britain in the late 1960s and 1970s gives us a window into how tough life was for many South Asians in Britain. They had to work twice as hard to survive. His story also sheds light on the social and community dynamics of South Asians living in diaspora, and the tendency to stick within family and cultural units.

Ram's religious background, including Hinduism, Sikhism and Islam, reveals the complex religious worldview of South Asians. This complexity is often overlooked by Christians who, in ignorance, have no clue that it is not always easy to convert from these religions because of family and community exclusions that often await those who dare to do so. But there is also the matter of theological and worldview differences between Hinduism and Christianity which pose a lot of challenges for many South Asians. Ram, however, after converting to Christianity, was able to see beyond this divergence to the affinities between Hinduism and Christianity. He inculturated concepts of sacrifice from the Verdic tradition to understand the atonement in the Bible, which one could say led Ram to develop a systematically Asian Theology. This enabled him to communicate the gospel to his family and South Asians in Britain. It is something worth celebrating as it is a pioneering effort and an attempt to contextualise the gospel for South Asians in Britain.

Ram took a holistic approach, in what would be regarded as integral mission, in engaging with issues affecting South Asians in Britain and India. These issues include poverty, family dislocation and the failure of British churches to reach out to or understand South Asians in their midst. This led him and three other pioneers to start South Asian Concern, which developed missional communities known as Masala for South Asians in Britain. This undertaking was combined with relief work.

Another important thing about Ram's ministry is that he did not limit and restrict himself to his own people; he sought partnership with the wider British populace. This is exemplified in his work with Steve Chalke when they started the Christmas Cracker initiative in 1988 which was very fruitful. Ram's story also demonstrates how a Christian entrepreneur can use his or her skills for the sake of God's kingdom. His business acumen and strategy went a long way to developing the various Christmas Cracker projects and other organisations' initiatives. Ram's story teaches us that although it is a good idea for people to own their problem and respond, it is still important to integrate and form meaningful partnerships with other people who can also help.

Chapter Nine
Sri Lankans in London
Harry Tennakoon

The psalmist, King David, says:

> For you created my inmost being; you knit me together in my mother's womb... Your eyes saw my unformed body; all the days ordained for me were written in your book before one of them came to be.' (Psalm 139:13, 16)

When I was a Buddhist, I was not taught this kind of reality about my life. I was taught that I am being reincarnated and that I may have many thousands of births during the existence of the world. Buddhists are not properly taught about an end to the world either, meaning that this cycle of reincarnation could seem interminable. Because of the 'demerits' we have done, we will be reincarnated in many lives and, in each of those lives, we have to pay the price for our demerits, for our sins. This is like the wheel of a bullock cart rolling behind the bull: all our sins will follow us over and over again in each of our births. There is no guarantee that a man will be born as a man in his next birth; he may be born as any creature, eg a fly, a worm, a dog or a pig.

A young Sri Lankan lady conceived, and the pills she took to wash out the embryo failed. That became another worry for her; firstly she worried about the conception (which was unlawful, or outside of marriage, because her boyfriend had deceived her and run away), and secondly she worried deeply because the embryo had not been washed out and therefore she thought that she would deliver a handicapped child into the world.

On the eighth day of May 1960 she delivered a child. She was amazed; the child was perfect and more beautiful than any other child she had ever seen in her life. She had not known that this child had been knitted into her womb by the maker of the heavens and the earth. But David knew it. That's why he wrote that psalm. Do you know who this child is? Probably not!

When an unbeliever or a non-Christian examines this child's life, they will not observe the unseen hand protecting him in his childhood, but I do. 'Where can I go from your Sprit? Where can I flee from your presence? ... Your right hand will hold me fast' (Psalm 139: 7, 10).

The above lady had to get married two years after delivering this child, and she had to take the child to her new house to live with her and her husband. A few months later, she returned from her allotment one day and felt that the child was in fear and not behaving normally. She thought that perhaps the child had not been fed properly by his stepfather, and therefore she raised his little shirt to see his belly. She screamed. The child was burnt and the whole belly area was red and full of blisters.

After about three months of native treatments, the child recovered. This was his second life-threatening situation, or in other words, his second escape from death.

Another time, when this child was about seven years old, a car hit him. He rolled from one side of a major road to the other, but he did not have even a scratch on his body. This was his third miraculous escape.

This reminds me of Joseph's story in the Old Testament. When Joseph's brothers were trying to kill him, his eldest brother saved him and instead they put him into a pit. When Joseph was serving his master in Egypt, his mistress told a false story and put him into a prison. But finally God delivered him from all evil and made him the second in command in Egypt (Genesis 37–48).

The child in Sri Lanka was brought up by his grandparents after he was burnt, and he was treated better and given a better education than any of the other members of the family. Some family members were jealous of him. They all were villagers who lived in a remote rural area of Sri Lanka.[69]

This child was very blessed among all his relatives, and he was offered the opportunity by one of his uncles to go to Colombo (the

---

[69] The village is called Galapitagala, which is about 125 miles away from Colombo. They did not have proper transport facilities, education, medical treatments, electricity, and communication facilities in 1960s.

capital of Sri Lanka) for his higher studies. After his A Levels, he met his fiancée in a work place in 1984. She had already converted to the Christian faith during her university days. With her influence, this young man too got to know Jesus through Campus Crusade for Christ on 12th December 1988 at 5.30pm in their headquarters in Colombo.

Looking back at this man's life till this moment, surely there has been a mighty unseen hand over him. After a few months as a born-again Christian, he moved to England and there he graduated with a Bachelor of Theology degree from the University of Wales. He is now the pastor of United Sri Lankan Christian Fellowship in Whyteleafe, a small village in Surrey. His name is Harry Tennakoon, and I am he.

Harry's experience of cross-cultural missions in the UK

The United Kingdom is one of the major multicultural countries in the world, and I believe this is a blessing from God. If there are around 6,909 languages in the world,[70] then it is likely that all these languages will be spoken in the United Kingdom and all their nationalities will be represented here. The problem is that even if all these people spoke English, they would still come from 6,909 different cultures. How can the English have churches to suit all these cultures? I think it is totally impossible. The next question is, who is responsible for their spiritual lives?

One day, one of the new believers in a Bible study group asked, 'Why did God come to the earth as a man? Why he did not appear as an angel or as God Himself?' Then my teacher, Bro Oswald Salgado,[71] said, 'If when a man is digging or ploughing his land for cultivation, he sees a herd of ants ahead, and if he wants to let them move out of his way, can he tell them to do so? Or in other words, can the man speak in ants' language and convince them to move

[70] http://lsadc.org/info/ling-faqs-howmany.cfm (accessed 5 August 2013).
[71] Oswald Salgado is now the Head of Campus Crusade for Christ in Sri Lanka. He is the one who led me to Christ.

away? It is not possible for him at all. So, what is the most suitable way to move them then? Either he should learn ants' language or he should become an ant to lead them away. Similarly, if God had come as an angel, probably people will not believe Him, or run away. That is why, as the final resort, God became a man to speak to man.'

Similarly, I believe that the different cultures in the UK should have their own ministers to minister to them. This is because, even though English is one of the most popular international languages, the way and manner in which people from different cultures and ethnicities pronounce English and use English words are different. For instance, Londoners' accents are different to Liverpudlians' or those of Northern Ireland. Besides, many of the cultures living in the UK have their own native languages.

I was invited by a pastor who is pastoring more than 3,000 people in London to conduct a service within his church in my own language. My language is Sinhalese and this pastor's language is Tamil, but we are both are from the same country – that is, Sri Lanka. This pastor had noticed that some Sinhalese people were attending his Tamil services just because they loved the cultural music, worship style and preaching style. But he was not comfortable about ministering to them because he could not speak to them in the Sinhalese language, or in English because his English was very poor. Therefore his solution for the Sinhalese-speaking people who attended his church was for me to minister to them. This was very reasonable.

Honestly speaking, there are many nationalities living in the UK who cannot speak or understand English. I believe that our generation will never be able to learn English to the standard of native English people, but my generation know God and they need the support and encouragement to practise their faith and tradition so that they can pass it on to the second- and third-generation migrants who are struggling with faith. These second- and third-generation migrants are struggling with faith and culture because they are British born and living in a modern, rationalised world where atheism is growing rapidly.

After serving the Lord for more than two years as a pastor to Sinhalese-speaking people under the banner of Faith Church of God, we decided to move from there to start our own ministry in Whyteleafe, where we now reside. We started our ministry under the name United Sri Lankan Christian Fellowship. Our ministry can see the potential and the need of the Word of God for people from non-Christian backgrounds, especially those from Eastern religious backgrounds.

Our church meets in the afternoon in a free evangelical church. The support we receive from the pastor, Paul Raiseley, and the believers of Whyteleafe Free Church is remarkable. They allow us to conduct our services in the church using the chapel and all the instruments and equipment free of charge. Some of their members, including Pastor Paul, attend our services occasionally, which is very encouraging. Even though Whyteleafe is a village where more than 90 per cent of the population is white English, Whyteleafe Free Church is a multicultural church, with members who are Japanese, Chinese, Indian, African-Caribbean and Sri Lankan.

Finally, I would like to thank God for bringing us into this country as a missionary to witness to people for His kingdom. 'On this rock I will build my church, and the gates of Hades will not overcome it' (Matthew 16:18).

Reflections

Harry's background, like that of some South Asians,[72] is Buddhist, and he gave us some understanding of the concept of reincarnation in the Buddhist tradition. Harry's Christian worldview means that he sees God's providence as having protected him from his conception until now, and he has a strong sense of God having a purpose for his life. God, through His providence and immanence, was present in Harry's life even while he was a Buddhist. This is important in demonstrating a holistic spirituality.

---

[72] South Asia comprises the countries of Afghanistan, Bangladesh, Bhutan, India, Maldives, Nepal, Pakistan, and Sri Lanka.

One of Harry's key questions, which is important to consider, is whether British Christians can provide for the spiritual welfare of the many diverse people now living in Britain. The continuing need for 'ethnic churches' indicates that this need is not being met. Harry's point should be taken seriously as it highlights the place and importance of mono-ethnic churches in British society. Harry is speaking as someone who is pastoring an ethnic church, a Sinhalese-speaking congregation, and his experiences seem to have informed his view that someone has to look out for his own people or else they will be neglected. Harry differs from other contributors by asserting that it is best for Christians to be led by people from their own ethnic group, given cultural differences and idiosyncrasies. He states that it is impossible for British churches to cater for all the different nationalities present in the UK. This is very interesting, as it contrasts with the view that we should sacrifice and be prepared to compromise to build multicultural churches.

Harry also highlights the difference in the way white British indigenes use and pronounce the English language compared to those for whom English is their second language. This is important in any multicultural context as it brings to the fore the issues of awareness and otherness.

Harry is also concerned about the second- and third-generation South Asians who are born in this country. While they might be able to speak better English than their parents, they are losing their faith and the culture and traditions of their heritage due to aggressive secularism. This is a shared concern for other ethnic minority Christians in Britain. It is interesting that Harry thinks churches of one's own ethnicity will help second- and third-generation migrants in their faith, as some others assert that later generations are more integrated into British society and so not so interested in attending churches with the culture and traditions of their ethnic group.

Harry's church is very significant as it is well equipped and experienced to minister to those who are from a South Asian background. This is not something every church in the UK can do. While Harry's church is a predominantly South Asian church, they have managed to work in partnership with a white-led independent evangelical church. Part of this partnership is that Harry's church shares a building with them. This reflects the many building-related partnerships between British churches and ethnic minority churches. While some of these have remained as simply *a landlord–tenant relationship, others, such as Harry and Pastor Paul's, have developed a meaningful and productive partnership. It is very encouraging that Pastor Paul's church has decided not to charge Harry's church money to use their premises – this is a sign of real partnership and support. This example is very important for the future of ecumenism in this country.*

SECTION D

CARIBBEAN

Caribbean pioneers:
Philip Mohabir: an Apostle to Britain
a tribute by Israel Olofinjana

A brief reflection
Bishop Donnett Thomas'

A reluctant missionary: a personal reflection
Dotha Blackwood

Reverse mission:
towards a structural change in society
Joel Edwards

Chapter Ten
Caribbean pioneers

Philip Mohabir: an apostle to Britain
a tribute by Israel Olofinjana

A brief reflection
Bishop Donnett Thomas'

Introduction

This chapter considers the pioneering efforts of two Caribbean people. The first, Philip Mohabir, is now deceased, while the second, Bishop Donnett Thomas, is still living and ministering. They are both pioneers when it comes to inter-cultural ecumenism and engagement.

It is worth noting that Philip Mohabir's ministry influenced and set the stage for ministers and ministries such as that of Bishop Donnett Thomas.

Depending how you position Guyana geographically and culturally, Philip's story could come under the South American section or the Caribbean section of this book.

Philip Mohabir's story is written here as a tribute to his immense contribution as a pioneer of reverse mission, while Bishop Donnett Thomas' is her own short reflection about her journey in ministry.

Philip Mohabir: an apostle to Britain
A tribute by Israel Olofinjana

A tribute

Philip Mohabir was one of the pioneers of the black church in Britain, and his immense contribution to the Christian landscape here and in other parts of the world is unparalleled. Philip was one of those great church leaders whom God sends at a particular time for a specific reason. Just as God used Paul in the New Testament to pioneer a ministry to the Gentiles and expound on the teachings of the church, and used Augustine to develop the theology of the church in the fourth century, so God used Philip Mohabir to pioneer reconciliation between black and white churches in Britain in the 1980s. Also among his pioneering work is the founding of a cooperative village in Guyana (Hauraruni Village); the establishment of an apostolic network of churches in Britain known as Connections; church planting in Britain, different parts of Europe and the Caribbean; and the founding of the African Caribbean Evangelical Alliance (ACEA) in Britain.

Philip Mohabir was born in Georgetown, Guyana, in 1937 into a Hindu family, and had six brothers and two sisters. From around the age of ten Philip was trained by the Hindu priest in the village to become a priest, but something happened in a religious education class at school that would change the course of his life. Out of interest, Philip had decided to study the life of Christ as one of his subjects. On one particular day the teacher asked Philip to read Mark 1:14-19. As Philip began to read he sensed an unusual presence which he had never felt before. This experience eventually led to his salvation.

Not long after dropping the bombshell to his family about his conversion to Christianity, Philip sensed a call to be a missionary to England. After many struggles with himself, his family and his community as they came to terms with his call to a foreign country, Philip came as a missionary to England in 1956, sent not by a church or mission agency but by God's Spirit. His trip was paid for by his grandfather.

Philip came to England without knowing anyone or having any connections, so it was very difficult for him to find accommodation and to afford food. He went hungry for several days and slept outside in the cold on many occasions. However, Philip soon made friends with a group of white evangelical Christians and decided to visit the church that one of them attended. After visiting the church about three times he was asked not to come back again. He felt rejected and lonely and began to realise that the ethnic minorities in London were not accepted by either the society or the church. This partly sowed the seeds of Philip's later work to reconcile black and white Christians.

Philip began to preach itinerantly in Brixton in marketplaces, pubs and open spaces, as well as from house to house. Through this he met many black people who felt rejected by the society and the church. (It must be emphasised that this was not the case with every black person, as some black people were definitely accepted and welcomed into British historic churches such as Anglican, Baptist, Methodist and independent congregational churches.)

Philip began to help people, irrespective of their race, ethnicity or culture, in whatever ways he could, including feeding them, caring for them and finding jobs and housing. Some of these people who were touched by Philip's ministry started to attend the fellowship that he and some of his friends started in their homes. These house fellowships became churches and grew rapidly, becoming church plants all over south-east London. These churches continued to grow, meaning that they had to move from one venue to another in search of ever bigger spaces. Some historic churches allowed them to use their buildings while others refused, not wanting to associate with these 'sects' as they were perceived to be.

Philip and his team managed to rent a place where they all shared and lived together as brothers and sisters. This was a real community as they shared good news, ate, wept and fellowshipped together. This church community, based in Brixton, was multicultural as there were people from different ethnicities and cultures. Philip met his wife Muriel through one of the sisters in the church, and after about three months of intense struggle with himself he made the move and they started going out. Part of his struggle was the racial difference between them: Muriel was Jamaican, while Philip was of Indian heritage and from Guyana. He had to challenge his own racial prejudice and repent before challenging that of his family, and later that of the church in Britain. On 1st November 1958, Philip and Muriel got married at Stockwell Baptist Church.

Doors of mission in other countries such as Sweden, Ghana, Nigeria and Liberia began to open for Philip and his team. They therefore began travelling abroad, doing missions and forming significant partnerships. Their church in Brixton grew in numbers as more immigrants came to London. During this period, Philip met some of the leaders of the charismatic renewal in Britain, including Michael Harper. He also became good friends with Bryn Jones who was one of the pioneers of the House Church Movement. In 1963, Philip, Muriel, Bryn and his wife Edna all travelled as missionaries to Guyana where they engaged in church planting, establishing about 100 churches in total. Bryn and Edna came back to Britain after about three years, but Philip and Muriel stayed until 1983 when they sensed God calling them to leave.

Their return to Britain in 1983 was aided by Philip's new friend Dave Tomlinson, one of the pioneers of the House Church Movement and now an Anglican vicar. Philip began to observe that the black churches in Britain were growing in strength and independence at a time when British evangelicalism, through the so-called New Churches (formerly House Churches), was also becoming strong and relevant. However, they had nothing to do with each other. Philip became a bridge-builder and worked towards ecumenical partnership between black and white churches.

Philip's ecumenical vision became the blueprint for the founding of the West Indian Evangelical Alliance (WIEA) in 1984. He became the first director of WIEA, working with Clive Calver, the then general secretary of the Evangelical Alliance. Through Philip and the work of WIEA – which later became the African Caribbean Evangelical Alliance (ACEA) – the gap that existed between the black church and British evangelicals was to some extent bridged.

Philip also founded Connections – an inter-denominational, multiracial apostolic network of churches in Britain, other parts of Europe, the Caribbean, Africa and South America. The vision of Connections includes pioneer evangelism, cross-cultural missions, church planting, leadership training, relief work and racial reconciliation.

Through his ministry in the UK, Philip influenced a whole generation of leaders, some of whom are now in key leadership and strategic positions. He has influenced the likes of Lovel Bent, UK Connections Apostolic team leader and New Life Assembly's Senior Pastor; Joel Edwards, International Director of Micah Challenge International; Mark Sturge, former General Director of ACEA; Ade Amooba, co-founder of the Christian Legal Centre (CLC) and Christian Concern for our Nation (CCFON) and the Senior Pastor of Christian Victory Group; Denis Wade, Senior Pastor of Micah Church Ministries; Doug Williams, Superintendent of the London Region of the Assemblies of God; Rev Les Isaac, CEO of Ascension Trust and Founder of Street Pastors; Pastor Kofi Osafo; and many more.

After a lengthy illness, Philip passed away on 26th November 2004 in London at the age of 67. He is survived by his wife Muriel, five daughters and eight grandchildren. Philip wrote several books including *Building Bridges* (1988), *Hands of Jesus, Pioneers or Settlers?* (1991), *The God Slot* (1994) and *Worlds Within Reach* (1992). Philip will always be remembered by friends, family and colleagues as a loving father, a good husband and a genuine friend. He will also be remembered as an Apostle, a pioneer, a reconciler, a missionary and an ambassador.

Reflections

Philip's story is remarkable on a number of points. He was born and raised in a Hindu family and part of the plan was that he should become a Hindu priest. Through an encounter with a passage of the New Testament he came to know the Lord. What makes this amazing is the fact that there was no preacher who led him to Christ and discipled him, but all was engineered and done by the Holy Spirit.

Another significant thing was that when Philip sensed the call to be a missionary to England, God, in His providence, used his grandfather to send him to England. Philip was not commissioned or sent as a missionary to England by a church or mission agency, but by his Hindu family who were not sure what the call was all about. The brilliance of Philip's ministry in the early days was that he brought in a fresh boldness for the gospel at a time when Britain was becoming very secular. His spirituality and passion for God challenged people around him; this was despite the many sufferings that he went through and the rejection that he experienced.

Perhaps the most significant part of Philip's apostolic ministry was the founding of the African and Caribbean Evangelical Alliance (ACEA) (then called the West Indian Evangelical Alliance) to facilitate relationships between African and Caribbean churches as well as British evangelical churches. Lastly, Philip has also mentored and influenced many black church leaders who are today at the forefront of mainstream Christianity in Britain and beyond.

A brief reflection
Bishop Donnett Thomas

My father was in the Royal Air Force during World War II, and at the end of his term he had the option of leaving England and going back to Jamaica or staying in England and sending for his family. He decided to send for his family, and my mother and I arrived in 1954. Those were really hard times in London for us, as we had six people living in one room and also had to cook there. That was because people did not want to rent out rooms to black people, so we had to live where we were allowed to and do the best we could.

My parents were Christians and promptly decided to seek out a church where they could worship. This proved to be very difficult as most churches did not extend a welcome to them. After much searching they were welcomed by College Park Baptist Church in Lewisham where they remained, working in the church and my dad as a deacon until they emigrated back to Jamaica nearly 20 years ago. My dad passed away five years ago.

My dad was a pioneer in tailoring and was the first black tailor in the Drury Lane Theatre, and then he worked with Savile Row, Moss Bros and the Army and Navy store in Victoria. He worked hard and excelled in his job so that he could later return to Jamaica. His standard of excellence and pioneering spirit was something that I recognised in him and continued in my life.

Being the only black child in both my primary and secondary schools for many years brought personal suffering through ridicule, name-calling (being compared to an animal), hair-pulling (because it was a different sort of hair) and rejection by most of the pupils. It was difficult, but I knew the importance of a good education and was able to focus on that and succeed in my qualifications.

I later joined the Black Power Movement to have somewhere to place my identity because that was not available in the church. I had an empathy with my people all over the world and was always especially interested in Africa.

I am pleased that, as an Apostle and Bishop, God has given me the opportunity to minister in Africa through building and helping people. I have three churches in Kenya and one in India. Additionally, God has given me a vision for an apostolic network known as the True Redemption Apostolic Network (TRANS). Over a period of years this has been very successful in Kenya and now in London. This apostolic network brings together apostolic teams to network around the world, teaching and equipping those able to carry on God's work in their own locality and all over the world.

I am a president of the Christian Muslim Forum, an initiative of the former Archbishop of Canterbury, and I am also Chair of Churches Together in South London (CTSL). This is a great step as the first black woman Pentecostal bishop to hold this position. I have now found a warm welcome within the ecumenical movement in England where I have many denominational bishops as friends, and we work very well together.

I have seen a complete turnaround in the British churches' acceptance of people from other cultures. I now find it more difficult working with black organisations because some of them have failed to recognise that the church in England needs help, rather than to be overtaken and dismissed.

Reflections

Bishop Donnett's story is very powerful as it gives a personal and autobiographical sketch into the attitudes of the British traditional churches in the 1950s and 1960s towards black people. Bishop Donnett's reflection is an example of the racial discrimination in Britain during that period, when many Caribbean families were turned away from churches, rejected because of the colour of their skin.

Another significant thing about Bishop Donnett's journey is that, despite all the rejection and suffering, today she works within the mainstream British ecumenical scene through Churches Together in England (CTE). This is important to point out as it reflects that she has not held on to the past and resented, but has rather moved on from rejection to partnership. She understands that what is needed within the British church context is partnership as opposed to separation or independence, which she asserts typifies some of the black churches. Her concluding remark about the arrogance and independence of some black churches, although quite a sharp critique, is valid.

Bishop Donnett, as a Caribbean Pentecostal female bishop who oversees other church leaders, particularly in East Africa, becomes significant considering the fact that the Church of England is still to catch up on the issue of women bishops. Her contribution to the ecumenical scene in south London as a Pentecostal bishop is of paramount importance as there are not many female bishops involved in ecumenical work.

Chapter Eleven
A reluctant missionary: a personal reflection
Dotha Blackwood

These reflections are about how we found ourselves here in Britain glorifying God, giving praise to God, working in various capacities and being seen as reverse missionaries. Well, I will start by telling you that to begin with I did not see myself in that capacity at all; I did not see myself as a reverse missionary, or as a missionary at all. This is despite the fact that when I left Jamaica to come to England in 1993, they laid hands on me in my home church (I was already a minister of music there, doing all sorts of things) and commissioned me as a missionary, giving me a licence to act as an accredited missionary from the Jamaica Evangelistic Centre (JEC)!

I was born and educated in Jamaica. Most of you will be aware that Jamaica was part of the British Empire – a former British colony, and now a part of the Commonwealth. A lot of our schools and schooling systems were therefore very British in style. In my school, everything was to do with England, and I have the GCEs to prove it! So all my life, and especially during my school life, I was exposed to and encouraged to sing about England and think about the Queen. I shared at an international evening at Spurgeon's College many years ago that growing up in Jamaica we were taught the Queen's English, so imagine my surprise when I came to England and discovered that only the Queen spoke it!

Focusing on some of the highlights, I grew up in a home where my father was a pastor and my mother a teacher. It is said in Jamaica that teachers' and pastors' kids are usually the worst behaved – of course, I was the exception to that rule (yeah, right!). In my home we were accustomed to folk just dropping in from America, from England, from all over the world, literally – they would just turn up on our doorstep and we would welcome them. In my family we were raised to see everybody as the same; that's just how we grew up.

So the surprise when I came to England was to discover that I was black. I also discovered I was female. Now you'd think I would know that already, but actually what I mean is this: people started referring to these things as issues, and it became something that was thought about and talked about. As I've already said, it was not something in my context that we talked about or gave any special attention to – you just 'are', and folks just 'were as they were' when they came to us. This is not to suggest that there weren't areas, and even churches, in which this was not the case, but my own exposure and experience was positive, affirming and welcoming. Men, women, boys and girls were involved in the church and, as my old pastors often said, 'Whether you are red, yellow black or white, it doesn't matter; all have sinned.'

So in the church in which I grew up, we had people visit us from all over the world all the time. We grew up in the kind of church where you got involved as soon as you became a Christian; you engaged with your heart, your mind – all of who you are.

Part of our system had already been set up by missionaries, certainly from England and then latterly by Americans, who set up many different kinds of churches. I grew up in a Pentecostal church. When I first came to England and folks said they were from a large church, I asked what they meant and they said, '300 to 350'. I had to get used to that – the idea that in 1993 300 was a large church. My home church in Jamaica is about 2,000 strong. I had to get my head around this, reminding myself that I was in a different place now.

Why did I come here? I ask myself that all the time! JEC was the kind of church that did evangelistic crusades (as we called them then – under the big gospel tent) and church planting. I was involved in music, choir, preaching and Sunday school. Sunday school was for all ages: we would come before the service and break into age groups and do some serious and sometimes intense Bible study before the service started. That was a part of the system.

In school (my head teacher was an English woman), we would gather in the quadrangle for devotions: singing, praying together and reciting Scripture. This was part of the cultural fabric of the schools and the nation as a whole at that time. I don't remember specifically when I learnt Psalm 23 or the Lord's Prayer, for example – we used to recite them weekly, in the good old King James Version, of course; it was just part of our oral tradition. In this stream of Pentecostalism we had one bishop and many pastors, missionaries and other leaders across the group of 11 churches. In a church, when 'the bishop' started preaching, he would say where his passage of Scripture was from and put his hand behind his ear and listen for the congregation to finish quoting the text! So we grew up learning Scripture and being involved. Part of who we were – and are – as a Christian was studying God's word and also passing it on, so that was all I ever did – study God's word and pass it on, whether in speech, song or music.

I am a drummer and I played professionally for most of my life prior to coming to England. I left school, went to music school, learned, started working somewhere and then an offer would come to play on tour, and I'd be gone. I was travelling all over the world to various conferences, groups, productions, pantomimes and Broadway-type musicals such as *Cats* and *Grease*. But I always looked forward to going home; two days before the end of a tour I would be thinking, 'Yes, home to Jamaica! Wonderful! Lovely!'

I had no intention, none whatsoever, of emigrating or migrating anywhere, least of all to England! I'll share with you a little secret about the perception some Jamaicans had, and still have, of England. As kids, what we used to say about the English was that 'You're all mad – the crazy English!' Anyone who came from England to Jamaica acted kind of crazy in our eyes. One of the things was that they used to walk so fast; even when it was boiling hot, they would speak and walk very quickly! We would see them scurrying down the road and say, 'Look, the mad English!'

The other perception was that it was always grey, cold and wet in England. So just imagine – grey, cold, wet, mad people! Naturally, I wanted nothing to do with you all! God has a sense of humour. One of my philosophies in life is that, 'if you fight with God and win, you lose'. So fight against God, *if you must* – just make sure you lose the fight!

One of the things we did as a church was to link up with International Accelerated Missions (IAM), a Bible training institution whose headquarters were in Albany, New York. IAM set up six-month intensive training programmes to train people for mission and evangelism within different local areas. These schools are set up all over the world, and one was set up with us in Kingston. I was part of the initial team, as a student and a teacher, and then I was asked to lead the training programme when the original tutors left. This was alongside working full-time, of course (today we may refer to this as bi-vocational ministry).

Being bi-vocational was normal for us in Jamaica: you worked to pay your way through, or, more accurately, you worked to keep the roof over your head so that you could afford to work for God. More often than not the church could not afford to pay what one might call a proper salary, so you kept working and worked full-time at church as well. I was running the Bible school and working in a bank, and sometimes now I reflect and wonder how in God's name I found the time to do all of these things. As well as that, I was doing some music studies and learning to fly! Somehow I did it! (I have often thought that one day I would preach a sermon entitled '"Somehow" is God'!)

In 1989–90, after being on tour in 1988 playing drums in Boston, the Director of the IAM Bible school asked us to fill out a form which asked, 'Has God laid any countries on your heart?' I wrote England and Cuba. You need to understand that these forms were like all those at the end of a course that you kind of just fill in for the sake of it (at least, that's what I thought), thinking that nothing will come of it. Then I forgot about it, as one does, and carried on, already fully occupied, enjoying 'getting on with what God has called me to do and to be'. As far as I was concerned, God should be very happy with that. And I told him so! He didn't listen, though. (Another interesting titbit for the story to make sense: in 1983 Philip Mohabir, the founder of ACEA, had come to visit our church in Kingston and spoke there; and then I never saw him again.)

So in 1993 I was back in Jamaica, heavily involved in church, church planting, developing choirs, setting up worship teams, teaching, preaching and so on. My sister and I were living in our parents' house (our father had died and our mother was in the United States), and I had a car that I did not need to use all the time because I had access to company cars when the need arose, so my car was being used to earn some money on the side as a registered taxi – it was fantastic! Then I received a phone call saying, 'Do you remember that form that you filled in, saying that God had laid England on your heart?'

'Yeeeesss?' I replied.

And they said, 'Oh good, because we've had a request by a group of churches in London for us to set up and run an IAM Bible school there, and we would like you to go and head it up.'

I said, 'Yeah, right,' or words to that effect! I was just gobsmacked. I said, 'Lord! I just wrote that for something to put on the paper!' Or as John McEnroe would put it: 'You cannot be serious!'

So in early 1993 I remember saying to God that if this was really Him, He would have to do something to make it happen, because I certainly wasn't going to help. I pledged to do absolutely nothing to make it happen.

Seriously, that is what I said. That was around the end of February/March 1993. The next thing I knew was that I received another phone call saying, 'It's all been sorted. Your ticket is on the way, you fly out on 16th August. accommodation is sorted, all ready and waiting for you.'

'What? No!'

It was at this point that I needed to have a serious conversation with the bishop. It had been mentioned to him, but the bishop did not like letting people go. You see, I was like 'head cook and bottle washer' – one of these annoying people who are incredibly gifted to do many things. He liked having me around because if necessary I could lead, play the organ, bass or drums, sing, direct the choir, preach, lead the service... do anything that needed to be done, really. And now I had to say to him, 'You know this thing we were talking about? They do want me to go to England, and it is confirmed, and you did say I should pursue it to see if God would open the door...' I was dreading going to say this to him.

The IAM schools were for six months, three evenings a week and then on Saturdays from 10am to 4pm. We would pray and then go out on the street for street evangelism, witness and conversations. I decided that I could just about manage England for six months! So I persuaded my bishop.

At this point you would think that I would be interested to find out where I was going to and which church, but I was not interested. I thought I would just go and see what happened. It turned out to be one of Philip Mohabir's churches – New Life Assembly – and I was to live just round the corner. I went there on the Saturday and the minister at the time, Doug Williams, was there, and Philip was away. Straight away Doug said to me, 'Hey, welcome, fantastic, do you play an instrument?'

I said, 'Yes, drums.'

He said, 'Great, because we have a drum kit and no drummer!'

God does know how to hook us, doesn't he? So I arrived on the Saturday, and Doug told me to bring my drumsticks the next day. I showed up on Sunday as if I'd been there all my life and walked straight up to the drums. They embraced me; I became a part of the leadership, one of the ministers there.

I arrived on 16th August 1993, and on 31st August one of the group of churches, New Testament Assembly, was having an away day to Barry Island, and I went with them. My first impression of the sea in England was that it was about seven miles out and brown. We arrived there and the water had receded so far that you couldn't see it. Keep in mind I am from Jamaica where we are used to seeing lovely blue, clear sea water. I made the mistake of walking out and putting my toe in the water. Never again! I have not done that since; despite the fact that Frinton-on-Sea and living in Dorset for 12 years did restore some faith in the notion of 'England's green and pleasant land', with blue seas too!

Towards the end of the mission school we would always take a mission trip somewhere, so we went to Yeovil for a week of mission with a church there.

At Christmas 1993, I was visiting friends in Wolverhampton. I was in my friend's Nissan Micra on the way back to London when I heard God very clearly saying, 'I want you to go home to Jamaica and sort your stuff out, because I want you to come back; there is unfinished business here in England.'

I said, 'Oh nooo!'

A reluctant missionary or what?! I was enjoying being here in England – don't mishear that. I was just slow to get to grips with what God was saying. So I thought: 'No! I only said yes to six months.' But another group of churches wanted to send some delegates to the school, so I said I would go back to Jamaica to sort things out.

I wondered how I was going to tell the bishop that instead of the six months he had released me for, I was just there to tidy things up, pack a bigger suitcase and head back. So I said, 'Lord, you've got to sort this out.' I really was not looking forward to it.

In the end, the bishop came to me and started talking about one of his sons whom he hadn't seen for some time and what was happening there, and I said to him, 'Sometimes the Lord has to take our children away from us; sometimes he sends them off to be trained and equipped, and they might return some time, but sometimes we just have to let them go.'

He turned to me and said, 'We're talking about you, not my son, aren't we?'

I said, 'Well, yes. I'm going back to England.'

> In all your ways submit to him, and he will make your paths straight. (Proverbs 3:6)

One of the major parts of the story I haven't yet mentioned is that in 1993, when I told God I would go since He had opened the way and called me to England, at the same time my mother was diagnosed with cancer in the USA. I had already resigned from my job at the bank (they said they would keep the post open for me for six months), and now my mum had cancer. They discovered that the cancer had already eaten away the first lumbar of her lower back, and that the primary was in her thyroid. She had marathon ten-and-a-half hour surgery, and I went from Jamaica to the USA before coming to England. I had to decide, 'Lord, I will trust you. You have called me to England at this time. I will trust you to take care of my mother,' because of course the natural, daughterly thing to do would have been to say, 'Okay, I've left my job, I have nothing else to do; I can stay and take care of you.'

But God had called me to come here to England. My mum recovered from the surgery and continued to battle on, walking around again with her ups and downs for 11 years. She eventually died in 2004.

It was 1994 now and time to come back to England, and I was arriving from New York with a colleague from there who was coming to set up the second IAM school with me. I thought I didn't need a visa to come in; at least I hadn't the first time. So I arrived just before Easter and the immigration officer at the airport said, 'Miss Blackwood, would you take a seat please?' Now for those who don't know the code, that usually means, 'There is something going on here and we need to question you a little bit more closely,' or 'We are about to send you back.'

I said, 'Lord, are you going to tell me that after I wrestled with you and I finally said I would go, you're now going to say they're stopping me at Heathrow and I can't get in?'

To cut a long story short, my experience of passport control this time was that they were trying every which way to see how they *could* let me in! Seriously, rather than 'No, you just need to go,' they asked me what I was going to do and what my suitcase full of books was all about.

I had my diary for training and they said, 'Technically you don't need a visa; you need a minister of religion entry clearance, but unfortunately you cannot apply for it inside the country; it has to be done outside of England.'

I said, 'What? They told me I didn't need anything!' Then I said, 'Okay, can I go in to London overnight, unpack, pack a lighter suitcase and fly out the next day and sort it out?' Passport control are meant to send you back straight away on the same aeroplane, but they said yes! They let me in overnight. Seriously! They kept my passport, naturally, but people have done a runner with less than that. They also said I didn't have to go back to Jamaica but I could apply from New York.

I had to make four trips to the British High Commission in New York before it was eventually sorted out four weeks later. You can just imagine my conversations with God during this time, can't you?! Bearing in mind how I started by *so willingly* saying yes to Him! We had some really interesting conversations then. But as I said earlier, one of my philosophies is this: 'If you fight with God and win, you lose.' So I fought with God quite a bit, but He won each round. And He sorted it out, and eventually they gave me a one-year minister of religion visa that enabled me to do what God had called me to do. That was in April.

Now in August 1994 I was coming back from Leeds (it's always coming back from somewhere that God speaks to me, always in travel. Perhaps I should travel around a bit more to see where else He might send me to!), and on this journey God very clearly said, 'Go and get it down on paper that you know what you're talking about.'

I said, 'Lord, you know very well that I don't know what I'm talking about.'

'Yes, exactly,' He said. He told me then that it was about time I went and did some formal training in a recognised Bible college.

At the time I only knew about Spurgeon's because Doug Williams was there, and it was just around the corner, so I applied.[73] This was August, and college started in September. I had the interview and they said, 'Could you wait outside please?' Now they don't normally do that. (Are you sensing a pattern here?) Ten minutes later they said they'd like to offer me a place to start in two weeks' time! I accepted, at which point I said, 'Lord, you do know I don't have any money for this, don't you?' After all, I had just left my car, my house, my job, everything!

When I went back to Jamaica in February 1994 they had indeed kept my job open, but I told them that God had called me back to England, at which point my boss said, 'I remember when I interviewed you for the job, you said you felt God was going to call you to full-time ministry at some point.'

I replied, 'I said that to you in an interview and you still offered me a job?' She wished me all the best.

At this point I asked, 'Lord, I have no money. How am I going to pay for this course?'

I went to church on the Sunday and a lady from the congregation gave me a sealed envelope and said, 'The Lord told me to give this

---

[73] Spurgeon's College is a Baptist college in South Norwood, south-east London.

to you.' And she left. I had not told anyone apart from Doug Williams that I had applied to Spurgeon's College. When I opened the envelope, I saw that it contained a cheque, and the payee section was blank. It was a cheque for £2,000!

I said, 'Okay, Lord, you don't need to shout. I hear you; you do want me here! You do want me to do this!'

So I started my studies at Spurgeon's. I remember the first time I met the principal Nigel Wright and I told him I was a Bible college principal. He said, 'Okay!'

After two days of lectures, I was thinking, 'Oh my head! This is doing my head in!' John Colwell's lectures went way over my head! Then two days later John said to me, 'You need to do a Master's.'

I thought, 'Yeah, right. I can't even get what you're doing at undergrad level!'

God by His grace continued to send in all the funds and finances and supplied all that I needed. Towards the end of June 1997 I was still pastoring with New Life Assembly in East Dulwich and their church plant in Dalston, but I was coming towards the end of my studies. The church couldn't afford to pay me a salary; I just had a small donation each month to buy essentials. Everything else came by faith and trusting God.

I got to the end of my undergraduate studies and was continuing to lead, preach and train people. Someone at Spurgeon's called me to their office and said they had heard I was thinking of doing a Master's. I said yes, and they said, 'Okay, we'll pay for it!'

I said thank you and left.

I got home and wondered what exactly he had meant by that. So I asked again the following morning (yes I know, God does have to shout sometimes to get the attention of some of us!) He said, 'Yes, my wife and I were talking about it and we will pay for it.'

My response was, 'What, *all* of it?'

I thought (again), 'Okay, Lord, you really, really want me to do a Master's!' So I stayed on and did a Master's in Christian Doctrine.

Towards the end of that time, again I was seeking God. I should probably tell you that during that time I was working with other churches: teaching, preaching, setting up other training groups, all while studying. Towards the end of that time I thought, 'Okay, what next? How do I take this forward?' Someone came to me and told me that Moorlands College were advertising for tutors in Christian Doctrine and Biblical Theology and that I should think about applying. I asked where it was.

'Dorset,' they replied.

'Where is that?' I asked.

So I applied for the job and left the interview thinking that it was never going to happen. I thought the other candidates had it all together far more than I did. The next thing I knew, I received a phone call from Steve Brady, the principal, saying that they were unanimous and wanted to offer me the job – a full-time role as a tutor in Theology and Bible Studies, at which point I said, 'Oh no!' because now I had to go and tell the senior ministers at New Life Assembly that God was calling me to leave London and go to Dorset, taking me back to training and equipping His people for the kingdom.

Since that time He has continued to do that. My involvement with Spurgeon's College never ceased: I have twice been involved on the board of governors. I taught for 12 years at Moorlands College and have been involved at Spring Harvest for 12 to 13 years, including, for a time, being on the Council of Management. I have been involved in speaking at the Keswick Convention. I also still travel all over the place, sharing the gospel, equipping the saints for the work of ministry, building up the body, reminding them that God is a God of love, a God who says, 'I love you; My grace is sufficient.'

I think one of the reasons why God has brought me here for this time is to remind folks of the kind of God He is; to say that it is okay to be passionate about God and what He has done for you, that *God called you to be you*! Uniquely you! He did not call you to 'be somebody else'. He has called me to ask the awkward questions, or, as my sister often cringed about, 'to say the things others only think but would not dare to speak.' That is what really stirs me up! People ask me how I get away with saying things like that. I say, 'I don't know; it's just me!' God has called me to be me – not perfect; still growing in grace, but *me!*

I found out years ago that I cannot be anyone else. You know that good old Pentecostal preaching style, using 'halleluuuujahs' and 'the Looorrrd saaaaid, Godddd said' (in a very loud voice and accompanied by rocking backwards and forwards)? Well, I tried that once! It felt like everything I said just hit the ceiling and came right back down! And I said, 'Okay, God, I'll never preach again!'

And God said, 'Was that *you*?! I was trying to figure out who that was. If I'd known it was you, I would have given you some help!' I was so busy trying to be like others and do things like I had seen others do them. At that point I realised that God has called me, at this point in time, to be here, *to be me*, to bring a different flavour, building for the kingdom of God. And that's the long and short of it.

In September 2011 God called me again, full circle, to leave Dorset and come back to London to be a tutor in Practical Theology (Pastoral Theology) at Spurgeon's College, so basically I am back to where I started – training pastors, ministers and leaders to build God's kingdom across the world.

Reflections

Dotha's story is fascinating for a number of reasons. First, she did not initially see herself as a missionary. This was despite the fact that she was prayed for, commissioned and sent by her home church in Jamaica! In essence, she was a reluctant missionary. Her stories of hearing instructions clearly from God and responding with a yes (even if reluctantly) are inspiring.

Second, Dotha had a well-paid job in Jamaica and life was very good for her there. She had to leave this job and security to answer God's call to be a missionary in England. Like Rodrigo, this challenges the stereotype of economic migrants coming to the West for a better life, which is the picture usually portrayed of immigrants in the media and public discourse. In addition, Dotha could have resisted God's call as she had a legitimate reason – to look after her mother who was diagnosed with cancer. But she managed to obey God and came as a missionary to England in response to God's call.

Dotha's story also gives us insight into church dynamics in Jamaica. Some of these dynamics are the oral tradition of learning Scripture, Sunday school being for everyone and not just the children, and everyone participating fully in the life of the church. These are salient points, as many Christians from the Caribbean and Africa struggle, especially with the latter point, when they arrive in Britain, wondering why there is a lack of commitment among people in our churches. Some also wonder why some Christians here do not know the Scriptures very well.

Dotha's story, with beautiful examples of provision, highlights how God provides for His people when they are in need. Her contribution is also important as one of the few female voices in this book. In addition, as one of the few black women teaching theology in this country, her story becomes very important.

Dotha's ministry back in Jamaica and here in England demonstrates how versatile she is. She has pastored churches, played the drums, led worship, preached, taught, trained and equipped men and women for church ministry. She is a bundle of gifts!

Lastly, her context of ministry in England has often been in a multicultural setting or a white majority one. This is important, demonstrating again that some of us are working in partnership with our white brothers and sisters and making every effort to reach beyond our communities.

Chapter Twelve
Reverse mission:
Towards a structural change in society
Joel Edwards

There are three ideas I would like to reflect on in relation to reverse mission. The first is *identity*, the second, *influence*, and the third, *impact*.

I was thinking around a Bible story which shows God's missionary activity – the *Missio Dei*, God working in people's lives, the story of the incarnation in people's realities – that we can celebrate and study: the experience of the exiled Hebrews in Babylonia as recounted in the book of Daniel.

Identity

It is really easy to underestimate the social, political, cultural and ethical impact of the situation the Hebrews faced 600 years before Christ. They were taken to a foreign country, dragged away from their homes and their land was left desolated. They were socially re-engineered by this new culture, so much so that their names were changed, which was a big deal for them. Changing someone's name is a powerful social, cultural and religious act in relation to identity. For the Hebrews, engaging with and studying Babylonian customs, language and culture revolutionised their understanding of what it meant to work in this alien social, political and cultural context.

This was the reality for the three Hebrew boys in the book of Daniel. The huge issue of identity was part of the transition package deal for the Hebrews in what could be described as a missionary enterprise. They were not economic migrants, but they were taken to a different country where, on foreign soil, they still maintained a commitment to the message of Yahweh.[74]

---

[74] This story is found in the Bible in the book of Daniel.

When Enoch Powell opened the doors of immigration to Commonwealth citizens as part of the then Conservative government's policy and asked them to come and help to build the NHS, London Transport and the Black Country's coal mines, thousands came from the Caribbean. My mother was one of those individuals. She arrived in England in around 1958. I followed her, courtesy of BAOC – British Overseas Airways Corporation – arriving in May 1960, aged eight.

It was a humungous journey, and one of my party pieces is to tell how it felt to find myself plucked from one culture and plunged into another, arriving in London and thinking of myself as a British citizen, but discovering that I was a slightly different species of British than the Brits. That was a big part of the identity crisis for me as an eight year old.

An example of this culture shock was a trip I made to the cinema with my sisters somewhere in Brixton to see *Seven Brides for Seven Brothers* (I know, it was a long time ago!). In those days, they played the national anthem at the end of the film. When they did, we good black Brits from Jamaica stood to attention. All the white folks walked out! And we thought, 'What's going on? We thought you guys were British!' This was the cultural reality of the post-Empire Windrush Caribbean people who came to the UK and had to negotiate a whole range of identity issues: identity in terms of how we understood our own theology, our understanding of God, and how we then matched that with an understanding of Christian life and witness here in the UK.

I was only eight but I still remember the 'word on the streets' which was in my head as a youngster leaving Jamaica: 'Don't go to England because Britain is a *spiritual graveyard*. If you go there you will backslide.' A particular Scripture was also emblazoned in my mind as we worshipped in the English Scout hall where we cleared up cigarette butts and beer cans in order to worship on Sunday mornings. Over and over again, I heard this text: 'And who knows but that you have come to your royal position for such a time as this?' (Esther 4:14). That was a cardinal text in the hearts and minds of the Caribbean Christians as we came and implanted between the early 1960s and 1980s. Here was a huge issue of identity: what does it mean to be a Christian, and what is our mission task here in Britain? Primarily, we came over for economic and patriotic reasons, and to build a better Britain under the MacMillan era. But we were also asking, 'What really is our task?' And within that, 'What's our identity?'

When I came I arrived as a 'British West Indian', and a 'coloured boy'. Subsequently, I became an 'Afro-Caribbean', an 'African-Caribbean', and finally 'black British'. So the issue of identity has always followed us. Consequently, the African and Caribbean Evangelical Alliance transitioned from the West Indian Evangelical Alliance (WIEA), the Afro-Caribbean Evangelical Alliance, the African-Caribbean Evangelical Alliance, before finally regarding itself as the African *and* Caribbean Evangelical Alliance (ACEA). Behind these changes were powerful missional questions: what does it mean to be a black Christian presence in the context of British society? How do we do 'missions' in the context of that society? What does it mean to have our own particular theological culture? As a very strong holiness-Pentecostal culture, how do we mix a red-hot, four-hour-service and three-hour-sermon culture with the staid Anglo services going on? And how do you mix congregations?

Quite frankly, when I came to the UK, we simply assumed that black Pentecostals were the only true Christians! We thought Baptists were maybe okay because they baptised like we did, and so perhaps they stood a chance of being real Christians. Methodists confused us: we couldn't work out if they were Anglicans or Baptists. Anglicans had no chance and Catholics were the antichrist! We didn't even really trust white Pentecostals! They didn't preach for as long, didn't sweat, didn't jump or shout much and didn't sound Pentecostal! They just didn't look like the real deal. So for us, this issue of identity was a really massive one.

So I wonder how the three Hebrew boys coped on a daily basis under their challenging circumstances?

For the African-Caribbean, the entire experience was a mark of social, cultural and theological migration. Who are we? How do we do what God has called us to do, and how do we understand outreach and mission in Britain in relation to who we are?

A significant shock for me came when I went to London Bible College (LBC, now the London School of Theology) in 1971. It was an extremely significant time of learning and discovery. But for me, one of the great awakenings in terms of identity was to discover that God really had Methodists, Baptists, Anglicans and even Catholics who were truly authentic Christians, authentically 'saved'. By extension, this 'discovery' was of profound importance for our theological and spiritual identity as African-Caribbean churches in ACEA during the 1980s and into the early 1990s.

My own personal journey of awareness was greatly influenced by a very seminal experience while I was at LBC. On one occasion, a fellow student came along to my room and examined the small library I possessed. One book which dealt with the history of slavery was called *A Peculiar Institution*, and another, *Black Power* by Stokely Carmichael. These were two among the Anglo-theological books I possessed, but he pulled them out and said, 'Aha! Will the *real* Joel Edwards step forward?'

I thought, 'What does he mean by that?' I suppose up to that point I was fairly convinced that I was an Englishman with a deep suntan. By this stage I had the language buttoned down. I sounded English and understood the difference between fish and chips and rice and peas and chicken! That day I actually understood for the first time that others do not perceive you as you perceive yourself. And I was learning that this was also true for church life and missions. Others did not perceive us as we perceived ourselves.

Influence

Identity mattered to the Hebrew boys, but it is interesting to note that they were nonetheless influential. And I think it's important to keep that tension in mind.

Imagine the compromise they would have made on a weekly basis as senior civil servants in a wholly pagan administration. These 'boys' were totally Jewish, making a stand on the issue of food but still having to coexist with alien surroundings and to find ways of influencing culture as a part of the fabric of Babylon (Daniel 1:8-17). This was a part of their missional task.

The African-Caribbean church has also had to struggle with that reality. In the first instance, it is learning how it influences the wider body of Christ. And I think this is truly important. I am so pleased to see what has happened as reverse mission is taking place and more and more African and Caribbean Christians are slowly coming into places of influence in politics, business and in the church. Britain has a black priest, Rev Rose Hudson-Wilkins, who is chaplain to both the Queen and the speaker in the House of Commons. That is something to write home to mama about! But here, increasingly, are people who are beginning to have an influence: the likes of Jonathan Oloyede, Nims Obunge, Joe Aldred and Agu Irukwu – to name but a few – have become almost omnipresent in the life of the church and society in recent years. And it's important to note that this has become true of Africans even more than Caribbean people. The ability to influence has become a very important part of the black Christian community, and that is important for us in talking about reverse missions. It is a mark of the transition in leadership which is taking place.

The truth is this: it is much easier for a black person to be led by a white person than for a white person to be led by a black, Asian or Hispanic individual. That is principally a part of the social phenomenon of culture. Churches tend to reflect the social norms of their society. It would be a great PhD study to examine, for example, Baptist, Anglican or Methodist congregations where there was a 70 per cent white congregation before a black or Asian minister arrived, and to see the transition which occurred within ten years, flipping the ratio in the opposite direction. It is one thing to bring in someone from another ethnicity to 'perform' a kind of cultural presentation of worship, but quite another to call them to lead the host culture while still being true to themselves. Cultural minorities may influence to a point, but they are less likely to influence real change.

This has been true in my own experience. I would attend wonderful places like Spring Harvest, which I enjoyed for many years. But in my earlier years of preaching there, invariably someone would say to me, 'Preach it brother! Preach it!' and I knew what they meant. They meant, 'Give us that black Pentecostal thing. Run up and down, shout, do your thing, make us feel happy, then we'll go home and say, "Did you hear that guy? He was so good. Man he was noisy!"' But actually you are not going to let me lead you. I know this is a superficial and slightly caricatured form of cynicism, and that black Christians tell black preachers exactly the same thing, but I suspect that in the cross-cultural realities of the worship experience there is a grain of truth to be encountered and explored.

What did it cost for the Hebrews in Babylon to actually provide leadership as key administrators? And what does it cost people from ethnic backgrounds in reverse mission to be influential in the life of the church and society? It does cost something; there are parts of your own self-identity that you leave behind in order to negotiate a presence with people of a majority culture. And that's not about guilt, or about abandoning who you are. It is about a *dynamic interaction*, which learns that part of the missionary enterprise is to listen, share and be part of a dialogue of culture as we seek influence. And it is as black, Asian and Hispanic Christians are learning this that we understand the power of our mission call to bring influence to the body of Christ and the wider society.

It was quite a big step for the Evangelical Alliance in 1992 to say to me to leave my work with ACEA and become UK Director. This meant overseeing the work in Scotland, Northern Ireland and Wales, relating to other parts of the Christian community – people ranging from Lambeth Palace and Baptists to black leaders – and being something of a 'diversity officer' on behalf of the Evangelical Alliance. It was a very bold step to invite me to that role in 1992, and I discovered that it was also a fairly smart thing to do, because the Scots, the Northern Irish and the Welsh were able to empathise with the fact that a black fellow might understand minority feelings and the experience of what it meant to oversee a growing alliance with a cultural bias. In Wales, perhaps more than anywhere else, I learned the relationship between culture and identity. I learned for the first time the pain of proximity between Wales and England and the skills needed to negotiate that cultural gap. The experience of negotiating between black people living in proximity to 'Englishness' had powerful similarities. In this regard, the role of influencing the wider church of Christians in the UK became, and has been for the African and Caribbean context, a very important task.

Impact

Here is the last thing: how do we provide impact as a part of reverse missions, or across the north/south, south/north dynamic? The three Hebrew boys not only had influence; they really made an impact. In a religious impasse with the state, the Hebrews refused to worship the king's idol (Daniel 3:12). After the confrontation, all three of them said, 'Throw us in the fire; we don't care.' They had got to a place where their impact had increased significantly. The king was given to extreme behaviour; he seemed to be the sort of person who was either really with you or really against you. In this instance he went ballistic and the Hebrew boys wound up in the fire (Daniel 3:13, 19). When God took them through the ordeal, the king said, 'For no other God can do what this one does!' (Daniel 3:29, Living Bible). This was real impact. Because of their actions, the king decreed that structures would change, and the very laws and constitution of the land changed.

Impact goes beyond influence. I don't really care where you come from in the missionary enterprise, structural change is part and parcel of that mission, and that is a part of the challenge facing those of us from ethnic minorities. And I think this is about dialogue and partnership.

The thing I hope we don't do is see this discussion as one of those where the black and Hispanics tell the 'white guys', 'We're big and we're in town,' while guilt-ridden white people are thinking, 'If only we could have big churches.' That is not the issue. The issue we face together is this: how do we integrate together with God – black and white – in order to have *influence* and make a difference?

The ultimate result of eighteenth- and nineteenth-century mission work was about structural and systemic change. They influenced the health service, education and government. They improved infrastructure and built the railways. And because mission in these centuries was often linked to government enterprise overseas, they had immediate access to systemic and structural bodies. When William Carey, the father of the modern missionary movement, went to India and saw women being burnt with their husband's funeral pyres, he said, 'We've got to change that.' That is structural change.

This is good news. Similarly, the history of missions from the Caribbean goes back quite a long way. Black Christian influence here in the UK is not a new phenomenon. The Baptist missionary, Joseph Fuller, was a great Caribbean missionary, recruited from Jamaica at the age of 18. He came to Britain, trained as a missionary and in 1845 went to Cameroon where he served until 1888 when he handed over the Baptist Missionary Society to the German Missionary Society. After he retired, Fuller spent his last 20 years in Stoke Newington, London. Joseph Merrick, his contemporary, was responsible for translating the Bible into the local dialect. During this fruitful period, boatloads of Africans from the Caribbean and Nova Scotia arrived in Britain, bound for Africa as nineteenth-century missionaries.

These people were involved in transformation. I am not happy with a concept of reverse mission which is primarily concerned about the size of our churches, or which compares one cultural group against the indigenous one simply to talk about how fast we are growing. That is great, and it is great that in African, Caribbean or Hispanic churches we can all pray together out loud without confusing God in the process. It's okay to celebrate our decibel count in worship and intimidate poor white folks as a result. But what I am really looking for is how we get the Hispanic, African and Caribbean missionaries to become involved in *systemic and structural issues*.

Why is it that when we talk about poverty in Africa, India or Latin America, these groups are not present? Why do Christian Aid and Tearfund carry the burden of representing these structural issues in the absence of the very communities they represent? When will we see the next part of the task as building on our crucial spiritual agenda – the transformation of souls – to the *transformation of society*? And how will we measure its impact? What is the relationship between Colombian Christianity and its massive growth, Caribbean Christianity and its high church attendance, African Christianity and its massive growth, and poverty, injustice and corruption in those very areas of the world?

So there is a part of the reverse mission which has yet to be completed: the lack of *structural impact* which is a part of the mission's task. And if all we do in this missionary enterprise is to transport from the global south an understanding of missions which is devoid of structural change and lasting impact, then what I fear is that in the next 40 years we will see a mission presented from the global south which just replicates a kind of piety by which we coexist with the culture rather than seeking to bring lasting and powerful change to it. God is about *impact* as much as He is about influence.

The work that I have been involved with over the years has been a part of that journey. It is imperfect and inconclusive, but it is also exciting and downright frightening! No one has the complete or comprehensive answer, but what I've discovered is that together we are getting there. You cannot imagine the joy I now share here in the UK knowing that I am no longer the only black person who walks in a building of 200 people talking about Jesus; I am no longer the only card-carrying Caribbean or African in so many settings. God is doing a marvellous thing, and I hope that this reflection will help us to be workers together as we see the wonderful thing God is doing from the Caribbean, Latin America, Asia and Africa to enrich Christian faith in the UK.

Slowly we have become aware that we are here not just in order to resist the culture but also in order to enrich it. As the story shows, there is a place for faith resistance to idolatry, but these three Hebrew boys weren't primarily concerned to resist the might of Babylon – they set about *influencing for change*, and I hope that is what God helps us to do in the contemporary UK context.

Reflections

Joel's thoughts and reflections on reverse mission and the direction it should take are very profound, and should shape the future of the discourse. His contribution to this book is very significant in so many respects. Like Bishop Donnett Thomas, he represents one of the earlier generation of Caribbean people who came to join their families in the 1960s. He explores the issue of the identity of young black people in that period, and issues of identity are still very much relevant for the subsequent generations of Caribbean and African people born in this country. Like Dotha, he has found that people in Britain categorise him according to his background and the colour of his skin. His observations that white people struggle to be led by black, Asian or Hispanic people and that non-white leaders are often unable to 'lead the host culture while still being true to themselves' are very challenging and deserve further exploration.

Joel's insight on the history and growth of black majority churches is very significant because he was a part of the leadership of one – the New Testament Church of God in Mile End. He was not only part of the black church but was a major player with regard to the founding and development of the African Caribbean Evangelical Alliance (ACEA), becoming its second director after the founder Philip Mohabir. The contributions of ACEA to the development of black majority churches in Britain are immense, as it was able to draw together African and Caribbean churches.

Joel's observations and critique of reverse mission are important, as the direction he offers is, in my opinion, the way forward for those of us who have come from the global south. It is not enough to have megachurches and convert people to our churches. While these are not necessarily bad things, we must, as Joel suggests, move from influence to impact. We need to work to change systemic and structural issues in areas including education, health, economic development and the environment. These are issues that the black, Asian and South American churches must grapple with.

Joel is not speaking as someone who offers insight from an armchair; on the contrary, as the International Director of Micah Challenge he is involved in addressing issues of global poverty which greatly affect the global south. This is one reason why we cannot afford to stand back and just grow and plant churches, as there is work to be done back in our own countries and continents. Let us, like the three Hebrew boys in the book of Daniel, live our lives to impact both church and society here in Britain and around the world, for this is the goal of reverse mission. To achieve this, partnership with our white brothers and sisters is needed. Joel is a pioneer of such partnership as he became the first black person to hold the post of UK Director of the Evangelical Alliance!

Chapter Thirteen
Conclusion
Israel Olofinjana

The stories of each contributor in this book are significant for several reasons. All the contributors are involved in cross-cultural mission in the UK, and some of them also in other parts of the world.

They have all made efforts to bridge the gap, either by working in partnership with British churches (historic or new),[75] agencies and institutions or by ministering in a multicultural church or ministry context. This is significant, demonstrating that Christians from the global south are integrating and believe in partnership.

The critics of reverse mission have often said that Christians from the global south are only ministering to their own people (mono-ethnic mission). However, many of the stories in this book challenge that assumption or stereotype, from Rodrigo Assis da Silva ministering to many nations in Thamesmead, to Joel Edwards who was UK Director for the Evangelical Alliance. It must also be argued that there are historic as well as contemporary factors that have led to leaders from the global south 'looking out for their own people'. To use an example from this book, Harry Tennakoon's church is mainly Sinhalese-speaking, and part of the reason for this is that their spiritual and socio-economic needs were not being met elsewhere. Harry's ministry is therefore to care for his own people who are often marginalised.

What is reverse mission?

This raises the question of whether reverse mission, or turning the tables on mission, is only valid when white British indigenes are the ones being evangelised. This leads to the question: are only white people British? These questions are important, because if non-British

---

[75] In the case of José Carlos Lara in chapter three, working with churches in Northern Ireland.

people have moved from their countries and continents to settle in Britain, and many have become British citizens in the process, are they not British?

A related issue is that immigrants have given birth to second- and third-generation Africans, Caribbean people, Asians and South Americans who have been born and raised in this country and who will be considered British. If they are, then it is important that someone ministers to them as well as to white British indigenes. According to Harry Tennakoon, people from their own background are best placed to do this, although others disagree.

We must make every effort to reach out to all people – that is, white British indigenes and people with different cultural backgrounds, whether permanent or temporary residents.

Structural change

In moving this conversation forward, the goal of reverse mission has to be what Joel Edwards suggested – *structural change*. This is crucial for legacy and posterity's sake. As Joel describes, part of the contribution of European Christianity in Africa and other parts of the world was the building of infrastructure such as schools and hospitals. In a similar but different way, we must work towards affecting lasting change in society, including addressing issues of inequality and power. In essence, we must speak truth to power and be ready to influence government policies that affect local issues and global poverty. For this to be a reality it will mean that some of us will have to become politicians and advocates in different professional spheres, and encourage others to take up this challenge. Pastors alone cannot affect transformation in society.

Training and equipping

Another thing to consider in taking this conversation forward is what Peter Oyugi suggests in chapter seven – the need to train and integrate missionaries and pastors from the global south. Many of the writers in this book have learnt by experience the dynamics of cross-cultural mission and engagement. Although some of them have also studied, it has been mainly learning on the job.

Part of the purpose of this book is to offer a resource for new missionaries and pastors from the global south; one hopes that this will be a helpful tool in equipping and training newcomers.

Peter Oyugi recommends that missionaries and pastors from the global south enrol in some form of cross-cultural mission training. This cannot be over-emphasised, as it is important for the context of ministry in Britain.

Another way to help new missionaries and pastors is through mentoring. If those of us who have been in the UK for some time can serve as mentors to new pastors and missionaries, we can help them to learn from our experiences and mistakes.

Humility in the UK church

The third point in moving this conversation forward is that it is not enough for UK Christians to acknowledge and recognise that the centre of gravity of world Christianity has changed. This has to be followed by meaningful engagement that moves beyond lip service, realising that the UK church has a lot to learn from others. This is part of what Tayo Arikawe shares in chapter six, as he differentiates between multi-ethnic and multicultural churches – the former being diverse in attendance but with the power and church culture still white-dominated.

So how do things need to change? First, we need more Christians from the global south accepted into positions of authority and power within our church or organisational structures. This will include ecumenical positions. Christians from the global south also need to be present in research positions, teaching staff and senior positions within Bible colleges, theological institutions, mission agencies and seminaries. I am aware that this might mean that some of us have to undertake PhDs or further theological training; postgraduate theological study is something we have to take very seriously.

Second, it is not enough for people to write and research or publish books *about us* and not allow our own books to be published or *our voices to be heard* through the printed media. Black and ethnic minority scholars and writers often struggle to get their books published through traditional or mainstream publishers.

Vinoth Ramachandra, the Sri Lankan theologian, observed that most of today's theology is shaped by theological books published by authors from North America and Europe.[76] British Christians should be reading books by Christians from the global south and be partners in promoting southern authors. This is important because Christians from the global south have something to contribute, and European and North American Christians can learn from us just as we have learned from them.

Learning from each other is important as it allows for the coexistence of diverse theologies. Western theology is not sufficient for the issues that face our world today; therefore theologies from other contexts and continents are as valid as the ones from the north. This will mean embracing black theology, liberation theology, African theology, Asian theology, feminist/womanist theology and post-colonial theology.

Practical suggestions for both migrant and indigenous UK ministers

In conclusion, I want to suggest a few practical lessons that we can draw from the stories in this book. The aim is to help church leaders from the global south who are leading ethnic minority or mono-ethnic churches, or those leading multicultural congregations. Second, I want to give some practical lessons for indigenous UK pastors about what they can learn from the stories in this book and how they can build relationships with church leaders from the global south.

Suggestions for migrant ministers

It is noteworthy that many of the leaders in this book have made great efforts to adapt to the British culture in order to fulfil their mission. This means they have had to rethink the way that they did church and mission back in their country in order to minister

---

[76] Ramachandra, Vinoth (2011), 'Authentic Partnership: Empowering the South', *Mission Catalyst*, issue 4, Baptist Missionary Society, pp.4-5.

effectively in their new context. They have realised that there is no point doing church and mission the way they used to back home because the people here think and live differently. For example, I used to preach on public transport in Nigeria, but on observing the scene in London, I realised that doing this on buses and trains would be perceived by the audience as shouting aggressively at them.

To my African brothers and sisters in this country who believe God has called them to be evangelists here, please think about how you communicate the gospel in the public square. Ask yourself the question, 'Am I communicating to anyone?' A better way forward is to get to know people in our workplace, where we live and in our community. As we develop relationships with people in these places, we can begin to share the gospel with them by the way we live our lives and by letting them know we are Christians. I know this process is slow, but that is what Jesus becoming flesh is all about. Once people know us they are more likely to listen to what we have to say.

To pastors who are ministering among their own ethnic groupings, make every effort to build bridges with other churches that are different from your own in terms of culture and theology. This is what Harry Tennakoon has done with his church (see chapter nine). Harry sought out ways of engaging with the church that hosts them on Sundays, and the two churches have managed to work together and even have joint church services. Churches Together groups or other ecumenical unity groups in your village, borough, town or city are great ways to do this. [77] Why is it important to build relationships with other churches? If we do not want our churches to be limited to our own people, and if we want to learn about the British culture, then we have to build relationships with British indigenous churches, whether they be

---

[77] Through the Gather website www.wegather.co.uk (accessed 6 August 2013) you can find unity groups around the country, or through Churches Together in Britain and Ireland (CTBI) http://www.ctbi.org.uk/ (accessed 6 August 2013).

traditional (Catholic, Anglican, Baptist, Methodist, URC and so on) or new independent churches.

Another practical suggestion for pastors leading a mono-ethnic church is to try and speak English during church services. If we only speak our own language during our services, obviously this will not encourage people from other cultures to attend. This might mean that you need to send some of your pastors and members to enrol in an English class. Another reason is that if we do not want to lose our second and third generations who were born in this country, we have to adapt to the British culture by first speaking English during our services.

Some of the church leaders in this book are leading multicultural churches, and some of these are white majority in leadership and structure. This is not always easy, as we are pioneers working in a new context that we have not experienced before. An ethnic minority pastor leading a multicultural church that is white majority in terms of its leadership and structure presents a challenge. How do you ensure that you are true to yourself and your God-given abilities without white flight (white people leaving the church)? This reflects the experience and ministry context of Rodrigo Assis da Silva and Tayo Arikawe (see chapters two and six).

The truth is that an ethnic-minority pastor leading a multicultural church will have to be ready to sacrifice part of his/her identity in order to gain new perspectives and learn new things. In the process you lose certain aspects of your identity, but you will also understand who you are in a new light. Perhaps this is what Paul meant when he said, 'To the Jews I became like a Jew, to win the Jews' (1 Corinthians 9:20). To illustrate this, when I first started as a youth leader at Crofton Park Baptist Church, part of the journey I went through was to come to terms with young people calling me by my first name as opposed to showing respect by calling me brother, uncle or something else other than just my name. In Nigeria, young people out of respect would never call me by my name, but I had to remember that these young people are British and not Nigerians, therefore in the end I did not mind them calling me Israel. Another example was when I became an ordained minister at Crofton Park Baptist Church. The white people at

Crofton would address me by my name, while some of the African and Caribbean people in the church would address me by the title Reverend. A multicultural context demands losing certain aspects of our cultural identity and practices in order to gain new insights.

Suggestions for indigenous UK ministers

Some of the stories in this book highlight that many indigenous British church leaders and Christians recognise the need for missionaries and pastors from the global south to come and help in the UK context. This is why Tayo Arikawe and Peter Oyugi were both invited and called by their respective churches (see chapters six and seven). One suggestion to UK pastors who have the financial resources might be to invite pastors or missionaries from Asia, Africa or South America to serve on their leadership team, either on a short- or long-term basis. This will enhance any church or ministry as it brings an outsider's perspective to the UK context. It will also challenge stereotypes in Britain that people from the global south are all victims in need of help (an image which poverty charity work often perpetuates). Done in partnership, this will also help the missionary or pastor to understand the local scene.

In cases where this is not possible due to finances and visa issues, I would suggest short mission trips or short visits to be organised for pastors and missionaries to come from the global south. For those interested in hosting missionaries or pastors from South America you can contact Latin Link,[78] who also helped one of the contributors in this book come to Northern Ireland (see chapter three for the story of José Carlos Lara).

Another way indigenous pastors can learn from Christians from the global south, or build relationships with them, is to host an ethnic minority church in your church building, if you have a building. This can facilitate ecumenical partnerships that are meaningful, and be a blessing to a church in need of a building. If your church already hosts an ethnic minority church, the question is this: is your relationship with that church only that of a landlord/tenant or has it moved to a meaningful and engaging

---

[78] www.latinlink.org.uk (accessed August 2013).

ecumenical partnership? Do you know the name of the pastor? Do you think he/she is heretical? Have you held joint services? Does your church think your theology is better than theirs?

To those who want to move their relationship from that of a landlord/tenant to meaningfully working together, here are some practical suggestions:

- Do not assume superiority or have a proud attitude because you own the building. Instead have respect for the pastor and his or her church. See him or her as an equal partner in the gospel.

- Build good relationships with the pastor.

- Try and meet together to pray for your churches and the local community.

- As much as you may want that church to learn from your church, you must also recognise that you can learn a lot from them.

- Listen fully to the pastor and do not assume that you know everything about him or her or their church.

- Be aware of other forms of theologies and doctrines even if you do not agree with them.

- Build relationships first before questioning doctrines or theology.

- Be willing to learn and embrace other cultures. This must go beyond lip service.

- Encourage joint services that allow for easy participation and involvement of the pastor and his/her church.

- Encourage joint mission initiatives such as youth clubs, Street Pastors, food banks, immigration services and welfare for asylum seekers.

- Invite them to join local ecumenical unity groups that you are aware of.

To those who are not hosting any ethnic minority churches or do not have a church building to do so, find out if there are any ethnic minority churches in your area. If there is one, find time to get to know who the pastor is and build a good relationship with them, using the suggestions above.

God has brought pastors and missionaries from the global south to the UK to help build His kingdom. Building God's kingdom is not about those who have come from the outside building mega churches among their own people; neither is it about indigenous UK churches assuming a superior attitude and judging ethnic minority pastors and churches. Instead it is about working in partnership to achieve systemic and structural change in society. This, it seems to me, is God's kingdom on earth!

instant apostle

Join the Instant Apostle community!

Visit www.instantapostle.com and sign up for our newsletter
Follow us on Twitter @instantapostle
Find us on Facebook: Instant Apostle

Check out some of our other great titles!

A Book of Sparks, **Shaun Lambert**

Shaun Lambert weaves the ancient disciplines of contemplation with his modern understanding of psychology to unlock a biblical wisdom. Transformation comes through what he calls 'mind*Full*ness', the practice of being filled with the awareness of the presence of God.
ISBN 978-0-9559135-3-2

I'm a Christian – so what do I believe? **Ken Gardiner**

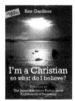

Ken Gardiner has a passion for Jesus Christ and a passion for truth. Drawing on his rich life experiences of God and his deep biblical knowledge, he invites us to re-examine the essence of the Christian faith.
ISBN 978-0-9559135-9-4

Building the Kingdom Through Business, **by Bridget Adams and Manoj Raithatha**

If it's business that shapes the world, then how can we use it to shape the world for good and for God? Against the background of an international debate on business ethics and more just societies, this book looks at godly business in biblical, historical and practical ways.
ISBN 978 0 9559135 1 8

A Thorn in My Mind, Cathy Wield

Cathy Wield is uniquely qualified to write on the subject of mental illness as a doctor and a patient. This is her testimony to ongoing healing and maturity while learning to live with serious illness. A must read for those who are affected by mental illness and those who run churches or communities.
ISBN 978-0-9559135-2-5

Ernie Gonzales: The Determined Dreamer, Beth Shepherd, illustrated by Lisa Buckridge

Ernie Gonzales is a small, ordinary snail with a big, extraordinary dream! Ernie sets out on a daring journey to find a legendary snail paradise and is soon swept up in a more exciting adventure than he ever dreamed of.
ISBN 978-0-9559135-7-0